The MUSE is always HALF-dressed in New ORLEANS

and other essays BY

ANDREI CODRESCU

St. Martin's Press, New York

Design by Charles Davey

Library of Congress Cataloging-in-Publication Data

Codrescu, Andrei
    The muse is always half-dressed in New Orleans / Andrei Codrescu.
        p.   cm.
    ISBN 0-312-09354-3
    1. United States—Social life and customs—1971–   —Humor.
    2. Codrescu, Andrei—Humor   I. Title.
E169.O4C62   1993   93-7441
973—dc20   CIP

First edition: July 1993
10 9 8 7 6 5 4 3 2 1

The following essays have been previously published.

AGAINST PHOTOGRAPHY; keynote speech at the National Conference of the Society for Photographic Education in New Orleans, March 21, 1991; Published in The New Censorship, *September 1991.*

ADDING TO MY LIFE; speech before the Conference on Autobiography at the University of Southern Maine, Portland, Maine, October 31, 1989.

NOT A POT TO PISS IN: MY LIFE AS A POT; Keynote speech at the 1992 annual conference of the National Council on Education for the Ceramic Arts, Philadelphia, March 5, 1992.

WHOSE WORLDS ARE THESE?; originally the introduction to Acid Dreams: the CIA, the Sixties and Beyond, *by Martin A. Lee and Bruce Shalin, Grove Weidenfeld, 1991.*

HAPPINESS OF THE MASS-MEDIA MAN (with asides on Death); published in Organica, *Summer 1991.*

THE THEATER OF OPERATIONS IN THE DRUG WAR WIDENS: DISPATCHES FROM THE FRONT; published in Organica, *Winter 1990.*

NO TACOS FOR SADDAM!: MEMORIES OF THE GULF WAR; published in Organica, *Spring 1991.*

HOW MY SECRET TWIN SAVED ME; published in American Film, *Sept./Oct. 1991.*

THE UNSURVEYED ARTS, THE UNSURVEYABLE ARTIST; speech before the Nevada Arts Council, Carson City, Nevada, February 1, 1989. Published in NEON, *Spring 1990.*

THE PRISONER OF PORK; published in Vegetarian Times, *July 1991.*

VEGETARIAN IN THE SKY; published in Vegetarian Times, *September 1991.*

IN THE RIO OF THE SENSES; published in American Way, *September 1991.*

SE HABLA DREAMS; Preface to New Orleans Stories, *Chronicle Books, 1991.*

All other essays are published here for the first time.

Contents

III: THE SUICIDE OF COMMUNISM

IV: CULTURE AND SPORT

V: WHERE I HANG MY HAT

I also found a little later—
I was growing up fast in those days—
that in the old cemetery
among the amputated angels and the listing urns
were ideal places to hide with a girl.
I hid there with Aurelia.
One summer afternoon she and I lay on the bodies
of two knights carved with their arms crossed
on their tombstones
who made a low sorrowful moan of long gone love
until we tumbled between them and there on the broken
debris we commenced the old dance.

I *Live Acts*

Partir c'est mourir un peu mais mourir c'est partir un peu trop.
VLADIMIR NABOKOV

It's hard times as they say
and Christmas is a dead season.
The wolves have their snouts up constantly
and you'll keep home if you know what's good
for you, if you have a home.
It's cold out there; for myself, though, strangely
the desire is greater to break out
of this space I inhabit in love's dungeon,
though the downpour puts a damper on my soul,
and there *are* a lot of bastards out there.
FRANÇOIS VILLON, translated by Jean Calais
(Stephen Roedefer)

Against Photography

UNLIKE MOST PEOPLE I WAS NOT BORN BUT *snapped* and I was not gestated but *developed*.

Both my parents were photographers. And both of them were Jewish. They were bad Jews because they were photographers. God said, "Thou shall not make graven images," and both of them did.

My father's graven image shop was on the main street in my hometown of Sibiu (or Hermannstadt) in central Transylvania, Romania. My father did all the graduation portraits of the local high schools and technical schools, and also weddings and portraits. The graduating classes posed for group portraits that were then displayed in shop windows up and down the main street. Marrying couples came into the shop directly from City Hall. When I graduated from high school, I refused to wear the school uniform in the class picture. I was the only one out of fifty people who didn't wear a tie. And I insisted that my pseudonym be used under my picture rather than the name I suffered years of school with. My father's shop was long gone by the time I graduated— as was my father—but I was driven. When our portrait was displayed, people remarked: "He changed his name, and isn't wearing a tie because he's mad at his father!" And my father, in turn, had been mad at God, which is why he made pictures.

My mother and father spent most of the six months that they were married to each other in the darkroom of the photo shop. I was no doubt conceived in the darkroom. And afterwards, I baked there inside my mother under the steady red light for six full months, the time I believe that it takes most major organs and most of the brain to form. My outline must have been there in any case, as well as certain vital shadows. I was then violently wrenched into the light by my parents' divorce.

My mother did not get her own photo shop off the ground until two months after I was born. I spent those two months in the sunlight with the family of a policeman while my mother got herself on her feet. These people were pagan. They were sun worshippers who slapped me when I complained about the brightness of the sun. "Don't ever say anything like that about the sun again!" the policeman warned me. I couldn't wait to get back into the darkroom again. Even today, I live in cities of the night like New Orleans, and don't fully come to life until sundown.

My mother's photo studio was called Baby Photo. (My mother's nickname was Baby, a very chic moniker in Romania where the word was redolent of exotic fragrance, bubble gum, nylons and big bands, a whole jazzy postwar longing that never materialized because the Russians came instead of the Americans. . . . but that's another story).

Baby Photo was at the very end of the central street by the train station and the clientele wasn't as upscale as my father's. Mother photographed soldiers and their girlfriends, Gypsies and peasant grandfathers brought in by their families from the countryside to be photographed before they died.

I grew up playing in the shop, and being photographed. I was my mother's favorite subject. She squeezed me into leather *spielhosen* and velveteen shirts, and had me stand with one leg up on a lace-covered pedestal with my elbow on my raised knee and my head perched sideways on my hand. This elaborate and unnatural position involved the creation of a correct face that my mother coaxed from me by threats, insults, endearments and sometimes—when it failed to materialize—by tears. "Don't make that face!" she'd begin, clicker in hand to the right of the huge camera that dwarfed her, "that's an ugly face! You look like a butcher! Don't grin like that! Why do you punish your mother with those rolling eyes! Is this why I was born? So my child can make a face like that?"

Amid the laments and the curses my seven-year-old brain raced through the muscles of my face in search of both the appropriate configuration and the most inappropriate because, let's face it, I was delighted by the attention, by the complete critique of any face I chose to invent. I knew the face that "looked like a butcher," the mug that "broke your mother's heart," the countenance that made her question her existence. It was all there, the ontology and eschatology of mother before the son in search of the photographable mug. At long last, the clicker clicked and I was captured.

Stiff, cramped, in pain, insecure and exhausted I stand there in the early 1950s looking at a point in the future when I would be released. That point came soon after Stalin died, in 1953, when the whole world behind the Iron Curtain let out a great sigh of relief and everyone's face muscles relaxed slightly. Some even smiled. Stalin's portrait, which adorned every building and dwarfed every school wall, came down. In its stead, other pictures took up the space. Our mono-pictural black-and-white world gave reluctant way to a serial picture world with hints of color in it. Of course, it wasn't until I left Romania in 1965 that I realized that the world could be multi-imaged and color-explosive, and that people could actually wear unconstrained faces.

Those early fifties photo sessions left me with a permanent terror of cameras. Whenever someone points one at me now I run automatically through a repertoire of faces before I settle on the one I have approximately decided is correct. It doesn't really matter who's behind the camera; there is only one photographer, my mother. And so to the question of somewhat larger import, "who's watching?" I can truthfully answer, "my mother," and I believe that this is the case for most people whether their mother was a photographer or not. Mothers watch. And, as John Ashbery put it in a poem: "All things are tragic when a mother watches."

There is also only one photograph: Stalin's, and that is the other story. My mother may have photographed me but the end product was a picture of Stalin. In those days, Stalin was everything. If you asked a schoolchild what two plus two were, he answered: "Stalin." Likewise, if you handed someone a picture of their recently departed grandmother and asked who they were seeing, they said: "Stalin." There was no one else. Given the elementary authority of that world, as well as certain subsequent developments, I can never believe that photography is in any way "objective." The photographer, who is the watcher, is always the parent, the subject is always the child, and the end result is always Stalin. And Stalin resembles the photographer more than he resembles the child. The child, like nature, is only there to be used by authority, machines and the authority of the machine. And this result, this photograph of Stalin, is always tragic.

Among the arts, and for me, photography is the saddest. Even if I grant you that there are in this world photographs that are not photographs of Stalin, their effect has to be tragic. Photographs are the object of a pointed melancholy having nostalgia on one end and metaphysical despair on another. When it is people I look at in pictures, I am sad because they are not there. (And they are *not* there even if they stand right beside me.) When I look at pictures of nature or objects of any kind—though I am not very much moved by these, I much prefer faces—I am struck by their strangeness, by their impossibly alien existence. And all other photo compositions, no matter how formally interesting, sadden me because they are based on the existence of an ideal which, curiously enough, is the world we live in. Platonism did not truly exist before photography. Photographs make it clear that a tragically unknowable reality capable of leaving traces on photographic paper was once present. But these pathetic traces, no matter how skillful, are only an elegy to the real, a lament for a love long gone.

Baby Photo was equipped with painted cutouts: There were bodies of uniformed generals with gold epaulets for soldiers to stick their bodies through; wasp-waisted evening-gowned fin de

siècle beauties with a hole for a head where girls from the Stella
Soap Factory could stick their own; a park bench with a sickle
moon on a wire behind it on which sat a well-dressed Parisian or
Viennese dandy with his arm in the air—the young lady who
wished to be photographed with him slid under his arm and
rested her head on his narrow shoulder; there was also a beautiful
girl of that same era with an inclined head under which a young
man could slide his shoulder. In addition to providing men with
the uniforms and the bodies of authority, and women with the
curves and frills of *La Belle Epoque*, Baby Photo had a horse, a
mule and a huge rabbit for children.

In 1953, shortly before Stalin died, my mother landed a government contract to photograph all the Gypsies in Sibiu for newly
required identity cards. The job took two years, so between the
ages of seven and nine we had Gypsy families practically living
with us, occupying every inch of floor, eating, whistling, singing,
breast-feeding babies and quarreling. The decibel levels were astonishing despite my mother's assistant Radu's halfhearted stabs
at restoring order.

One by one they paraded before the cameras, men, women,
women with six babes in arms, old men and women, thousands
of faces, day after day. Before I left for school in the morning,
the place was already filled with a stormy rustling of wide skirts,
the clinking of coin necklaces, the echoes of playful slaps, and lots
and lots of giggling. The men had wide-brimmed black hats that
they removed only after a great many threats by my mother to
call the gendarmes (the pictures had to be full frontal) and the
women hid their faces behind scarfs or babies. When I came home
from school, they were still there, taking large bites out of fried
meat (they made fires and cooked in the alley behind the shop),
asleep one on top of another, and full of unexpected (for me)
glimpses of tantalizing flesh under carelessly lifted skirts. I studied
the breasts of girls barely older than me while babies suckled on
them and wondered secretly what it would feel like to kiss those
big full nipples. As my mother photographed their faces I mind-

photographed erotic glimpses of bodies at rest and play. I was extremely sorry when the project came to an end two years later, in part because I'd made friends with two Gypsy boys my own age who had no inhibitions whatsoever about spying on their sisters and who knew the best times and vantage points for so doing. A week or so after the project was concluded, I visited with this one particular band on the outskirts of town behind the railroad track but two days later they vanished, to my mother's great relief. She'd had enough, although for years afterwards, she loved showing her friends the shop register where she had written down the Gypsies' names as required by law. They had all named themselves after handicaps: There were hundreds of *Surdus* (deaf), scores of *Mutus* (mute) and *Orbus* (blind). Whatever their real names, they had managed to turn a perfect deaf, mute and blind mirror to the register. I was not surprised to hear later that the Gypsy identity card project was a complete failure. The Gypsies burned their ID cards as soon as they got them, and the government had to content itself with a census. Instead of photo IDs the Gypsies had numbers. That suited them fine. In the whole country there is now only one Gypsy: No. 3458.

These Gypsies had good reasons to feel queasy about IDs. No more than ten years before, only one year before I was born, they had been interned in concentration camps. All of them, with the exception of children, were survivors. Tens of thousands of Romanian Gypsies had perished in camps. They did not want to be photographed. They knew enough about the state and the police to avoid photographs at all cost.

My mother must have understood their sadness well as she clicked face after face. My mother, her sister, her sister's husband and my grandmother had crossed the Hungarian-Romanian border at night in 1943 to avoid deportation to the death camps. My grandmother's two sisters—my great-aunts—perished at Auschwitz. They perished along with millions of others, a whole world of faces that exists now only in faded photos. In 1936, a man named Roman Vishniac possessed of an extraordinary urgency, crossed and recrossed the borders of Poland, Hungary, Romania, and Carpathian Lithuania to take pictures of Jews. Braving incredible dangers, using a hidden camera, he roamed the ghettos and the shtetls, and secretly recorded that vanishing world. He took 16,000 pictures of which 2,000 survive. He smuggled some of the negatives sewn into the lining of his coat out of Europe to America. It is difficult to look at these images. It's nearly impossible to keep in mind that the people we see ceased to exist almost immediately after the pictures were taken. These people went to their deaths almost exactly as we see them: in the puzzle of their childhoods, in the perplexity of their old ages. We see them all: scholars argue through the gray slush of Europe; wide-eyed children look to their teachers, the Torah open in front of them; sages, rabbis, zaddiks, Hasids in flapping black vestments and wide-brimmed hats. The European Jews of 1936, my mother's aunts and cousins, had been marked for destruction. Vishniac's children, from Seder scholars to street ragamuffins, share a seriousness and understanding beyond their years. In the crumbling innards of the old Polish cities, the threadbare objects of poverty glow with a life of their own. Here is a peddler with two customers, bent over a coat, carefully examining the fabric. There is an incredible *materiality* to this coat, paradoxically suggesting its opposite, spirituality. When this coat falls apart, this whole world will go with it. Soon, human beings will also become things, to be discarded and junked.

Vishniac has said that he felt that he was on a mission from God. In that case, it could not have been the God that had said "thou shalt not make graven images." Or perhaps it was the same God, allowing himself a tiny contradiction within a larger and more terrible meaning. Vishniac's camera is on a mission, a calling that is the opposite of the camera of the state intent on recording every face within its authority. Vishniac's camera redeems in a small way the use of the camera in our century, a use, by and large, infinitely more useful to the destroyers of people than to the lovers of them. The camp guards at Auschwitz all had good German cameras. They wanted to show their children one day what their technology had accomplished. These children, their descendants, are today's tourists. They too are taking pictures for *their* children: pictures of native peoples in quaint poses before picturesque arrangements arranged for pictures by the tourism bureau (the framer of remnants of the real for picture-taking). Well, at least, one might say, tourists aren't *killing* anybody for a picture.

Is *that* the difference between tourism and terrorism? Tourists are terrorists with cameras, while terrorists are tourists with guns. Tourism is the civilian aspect of imperialism. After the natives have been pacified by force of arms, we finish the job with the cameras. It's no coincidence that both activities are called "shooting." It's hard for me to look at old National Geographics without feeling an anguished nausea. There they are, on display, the dead freaks of worlds we have destroyed. They've left forms behind for the use of the fashion industry.

In Rome some years ago, my family and I strolled about with cameras around our necks and baseball hats on our heads, looking for all the world like *touristi Americani*, which we were. It so happened that Aldo Moro, the former Italian premier kidnapped by the *Brigate Rosse*, had just been murdered and deposited about a street away from where we were, on Via Gaetano, halfway between the Communists' and the Social Democrats' headquarters. Hundreds of screaming Italian police cars took to the streets, and trucks full of carabinieri were rushing in from the provinces. One of these came to a screeching halt in front of us, and a police captain holding a machine gun leapt out in front of us: "What's the way to the police station?" he asked. In stilted tourist Italian I told him: "Go straight. Make a right. Then a left." He saluted, thanked me and they took off in the directions I'd pointed them in. Only I'd made up the directions. I'm not sure what exactly went through my mind but I must have reasoned that if the obvious tourist getup hadn't deterred him, there was no reason for me not to act like a native. And natives, particularly in Rome, answer at length any question you ask them, even if and especially if they don't know the answer. So—the camera, you see—is not a *complete* defense against the stupidity of the police. Both tourists and terrorists shoot what they can't quite tame. To finish with the camera what your grandfather started with the gun is both easier and harder. The souls we steal may be our own.

My own revolt against my father, the graven image maker, took the form of bursting into the crowded waiting room of his shop one summer afternoon and shooting my cap pistol. When the smoke cleared, half the customers had fled, and my father had me in a headlock in the darkroom, lecturing on decorum. He wasn't looking at me. My act had been revenge, I suppose, on all the faces my father *did* look at.

Years later, in 1976, I still hadn't received my American citizenship, though I'd been in the United States for ten years. My only piece of identification was a so-called "white passport," a reentry visa really that allowed me to come back to the United States if I strayed over the border by mistake or something. I never carried this for fear of losing it. I don't drive—so—no driver's license.

One very late night in California, my friend Jeffrey and I were driving up a country road in Mendocino country in search of a nonexistent address when the lights of something huge and unearthly were suddenly upon us. It was the CHP—the California Highway Patrol—and a tall cop strolled out with a flashlight and a shotgun. He asked Jeffrey for his driver's license, and then he came to my side and said, "ID!" Now the only ID I had with me was an autobiographical book I wrote called, *The Life and Times of an Involuntary Genius*, which had my picture on the cover. The cop took Jeff's ID and my book, and went back to his cruise mobile. He put his feet out the window and started reading. Eons passed. Billions of stars died in the sky over our heads. I slept. I had dreams. Summer turned into winter. At long last, the cop came back. He looked at me long and hard. He then tapped my face on the cover with his trigger finger. "Anybody can fake a pitcher like this!" he said. "Sure," I said, "but wouldn't it be easier to fake a regular ID?" "OK," the cop said, "*this time!*" I believed him. Every ten years now I produce a new autobiography with a fresh picture for that cop. Photos *para la autoridad! Flores para los muertes!*

When Jeffrey died later that year, in a different car, I had the urge to look at pictures of him. One of our friends had been shooting a lot of our get-togethers with his video camera. When I saw the tapes I found to my dismay, that instead of Jeffrey's face—or anybody else's face for that matter—my friend had "composed" shots out of fragments of trees, elbows, house tops and clouds. Another reason to find art loathsome—for its effects on dilettantes.

I tried to use my book for identification in banks, in supermarkets and at public events of various kinds where it was sometimes accepted, sometimes rejected, depending on the imaginative stretch of the guard dog.

My first book of poetry was called *License to Carry a Gun*. It also had my picture on the cover. I was standing with one foot in a garbage can on First Street between First and Second Avenues in New York where I lived. A few years later I got a job teaching poetry in Folsom Prison in California. The first time I presented myself at Folsom I gave the guard my poetry book in lieu of ID. He called his boss on the phone. A huge man with hands that looked like they cracked bones for a living came down. He looked at my picture, he looked at the title—*License to Carry a Gun*—and then cracked open my book with his knuckles, and read. He then picked up the phone and called *his* boss, a guy no doubt ten times larger who ate men's livers for breakfast: "It's just fucking poetry, boss! Just fucking poetry!" he said. So the picture was good enough, after all.

The moral from these two incidents, if you're looking for one, is that most people in charge of enforcing the law, still have no doubts as to the equivalence between pictures and reality. Consequently, we ought to keep postmodernism a secret.

I had a dream once that life and death were positive and negative photocopying respectively. I saw the DNA strands being copied and was reassured. In that light, we are all copies, but I am a copy in the most exacting sense, thanks to Mom and Dad. Eventually, everyone will have to work out the precise sense in which photography engenders them. For me photography presents the Oedipal pure, but that's just luck of the draw.

You could say that my relation to photography is that of photography to the world: I come out of it but I don't necessarily give back a pretty picture. The day I burst into the full waiting room of my father's shop and discharged that cap gun I took charge of myself. The smoke and the shots that caused panic among his Sunday-best dressed customers gave birth to the unphotographable self.

Two pieces of advice then to the would-be photographer: 1) Pay attention to the thing you photograph, and 2) Try to love it.

I hope I'm not obscuring the issues. There is a great place on Bourbon Street where you can take your picture in a jail cell. That's where I'm going.

And then there are clearly unphotographable things that you can see. In 1973 I tried taking a picture with my 35 mm. of my two naked girlfriends in front of a poster of the kid guru maharaji but the pictures didn't come out. I tried Polaroid. No go. The poster or the guru did something to the light.

In 1973, the year that the political soap opera "Watergate" mesmerized the nation, I wrote the following poem:

ABOUT PHOTOGRAPHY

I hate photographs
those square paper Judases of the world,
the fakers of love's image in all things.
They show you parents where the frogs of doom
are standing under the heavenly flour,
they picture grassy slopes
where the bugs of accident whirr twisted
in the flaws of the world.
It is weird,
this violence of particulars
against the unity of being

Despite my accent, which makes "f-l-o-u-r" sound like "f-l-o-w-e-r" and "w-h-i-r-r" sound like "w-e-r-e," and despite the ancient awkward problem of putting Judas in the plural—which I did out of the instinctive self-anti-Semitism in which I was steeped as a child—this poem gets at my feelings about photography with remarkable ease. The functional word here is "weird," which was the word with the widest possible circulation in America during Watergate. If being has any unity in the age of television it is weird—to say the least—trying to fathom it through the fragmented and framed instances of specific pictures. What is one to infer of American life—and inner life—by looking at the triple-chinned mugs and black-rimmed eyes of our elected leaders, our meritocracy, standing trial for trying to hijack American democracy?

It is now 18 years later—long enough for a young man or woman to have been born, grown and sent off to be killed in a war at the request of the successors of the discredited administration of 1973. A war, moreover, that was so well packaged by the administration on television that not a murmur of dissent penetrated the skillful wrappings.

I probably don't have to tell you that the taking, selecting and distributing of pictures is a highly manipulatable business. In the past four decades, and most intensely in the last two decades, the ideological education of would-be mind controllers has been concerned almost exclusively with the business of image making. I will give you a single quick example before I proceed to more intimate aspects of my poetry—which, whether you know it or not, you are here to hear discussed.

The so-called "revolution" in Romania in December 1989 was an event staged for television by Securitate—the Romanian secret police—and the KGB—the Soviet secret police. In order to arouse the masses, they produced a number of images for TV: the most famous one is the so-called "madonna and child" picture, which shows a young woman and child lying on the ground killed by a single bullet. This image was shown over and over on the TV screens of the world until the alleged murderers took on mythic Hitlerian dimensions. In fact, this was a fake produced by collaging a woman who had died in an alcoholics hospital with a baby dead of different causes. A bullet was put through them, and they were seen accordingly. This image was followed on Romanian TV by footage of Nadia Comaneci winning triumphantly in Montreal in 1976. The two pictures together said: "Here is the genius of our nation, nipped in babyhood by the monsters of the old regime." Other images were equally bogus: children murdered on the steps of the Timisoara Cathedral, an image which gave rise to the extraordinary reports that 60,000 people had been murdered in Romania, turned out to be a collage as well. The net effect of all this camera work was to make millions of people believe that they were witnessing a spontaneous revolution while a coup d'état was taking place. But in fact a revolution DID occur, a mass revolt that was hijacked via television from right under peoples' noses. Today, in Romania, a neo-Communist government hatched in conspiratorial secrecy by the police claims to be the legitimate representative of this revolution. But it isn't. It is the representative of "revolution" between quotation marks. The most immediate effect of image manipulations is the placement of "reality" between quotation marks, the creation of a fundamental mistrust in the evidence of one's senses when confronted with slick images to the contrary. The evidence of one's senses has at its disposal only a very clumsy, very old defensive language, while propaganda and manipulation command a sophisticated technical arsenal that make human beings seem evolutionary throwbacks by comparison.

Someone out there in the recesses of literature flattered himself a few years ago by saying, "I Am a Camera." I remember also the beginning of a novel by William Burroughs: "The camera is in the eye of the vulture," after which he proceeds to describe everything from the vulture's vantage point using an interesting speeded-up cut up language that tries to keep up with the vulture-speed of the camera.

Before photography was an art, with all the pretensions and baggage of that activity, it served art by freeing it from the conventions of realism. The camera made modern art possible by freeing artists from the tyranny of the eye. The crucial moment in the history of modern art occurs in the Salvador Dali-Luis Buñuel film *An Andalusian Dog* when a razor blade slides across an eyeball. Henceforth, art is free of the exigencies of reporting reality according to the eyes. That becomes the job of photography. Of course, it wasn't long before Man Ray and the Dadaists discovered that in the twentieth Century, "art" should be placed between quotation marks. Art with a capital *A* was dead as soon as the first picture was taken and a long process of debunking—still in progress—was in order. The photograph brought Art down from its pedestal and gave it to the masses to have fun with. Which left artists desperately searching for new specialized stances in the mechanically violated wilderness of representation.

When the violent subjectivity of early avant-gardes showed signs of being exhausted, being a camera or an eye became art's first postmodern obsession. Implicit here was a certain regret at having ceded such a useful description of reality to a machine, but also envy at the infinitely productive capacity of photography. In the 1950s, in the age of existentialism, when it became obvious to everyone that the human race was doomed by the A-bomb, it became fashionable to feign lack of feeling, a kind of psychological "objectivity" whose ideal practitioner was the camera. Some artists confused the workings of the camera with objectivity because it provided a metaphor for indifference, both the existential and the Zen kind. For them, the camera made it possible to conceive of looking at something without feeling, which is to say without guilt. The camera seemed to make vision blameless, it provided the act of looking with a possibility of innocence.

However—the camera is no innocent instrument. Or rather, the instrument may be innocent but there is no innocent use of it. There is no moral difference between a camera and a paintbrush. Both are—precisely—instruments. Nonetheless, the camera continues to provide the metaphor of objectivity in a kind of theoretical space. With the populist snapshot at one end and the military satellite photo on the other, the camera is as complete a topographer of reality as we are ever likely to have. In short, the camera has conquered the world and the world it shows us is the way we now articulate reality. Which opens up wide the possibilities of manipulation.

We now read the world according to pictures of it stitched together either by powers behind the scenes or by the technological process itself. In any case, the end result does not benefit the majority of the people for whom the new imaged "reality" is an opiate that extorts their energies.

In the second or third wave of postmodern difficulties with the image, which is right now, few people say any longer, "I Am a Camera." The last I-Am-A-Camera people were the punks, or rather the catatonic wing of the punks who resented mightily the wavy impressionist hippies with all their shimmering light and idealized distortions. The severest punks were strictly black-and-white and they moved as little as possible. Their drug of choice was heroin—the most photographic of all the drugs.

More to the point than I Am A Camera is my own case, which is I Am A Picture.

Because of its teasing relation to reality, photography can be made to convince people of things that aren't necessarily good for them. Pictures can lie, transmit propaganda and change the evidence of one's senses to the point where reality disappears. Photographs make it also possible to substitute images for reality when the dread of the real becomes too unbearable. That is, I believe, where we stand now, in our time. We are forcing ourselves to believe in the simulations of reality all around us because we are quickly losing the vestigial organs for direct apprehension of reality.

And while I have you here, I want to put a curse on police cameras everywhere. I hope that aliens, mucking about the ruins of our planet, run into *your* pictures, or at least into a full set of *National Geographic*s, rather than into the millions of dreary mug shots that prove that our world was a dingy prison-planet. It's a matter of degree, of course.

Adding to My Life

MY TWO AUTOBIOGRAPHIES WERE THE RESULT OF accident, but each one begins with the equivalent of standing before people trained in the judging of lives. In the first one, titled modestly *The Life and Times of an Involuntary Genius*, it is my mother before whom the impending story is about to make its cheeky and devastating appearance. "You're not old enough to wipe your nose!" my mother exploded. "*I* should write my autobiography! *I* lived!" That was doubtlessly true, but she would never do it. She had not only had too much life but she had such an active quarrel with it that she would have been hard put to find anyone to address her story to. I was twenty-three years old: I had had as much life as I cared to remember and my audience—beginning with my mother—was vast. There were more potential witnesses to my life than there had been people in my life so far—a heady feeling. I could add them all to my life by writing my life. Which is not why I wrote the book, but it was a thought. Furthermore, it was high time that I became the author of something I could call "my life" in order to get on with it. Saying farewell to my mother, leaving her story, as it were, was not simply a matter of individuation. It was also a matter of sabotaging her story, a less than benign thing.

Just before the book came out I asked my mother about a certain incident I had labored hard to render accurately. It was about the time she left me with my grandmother, the Baroness, in Alba Iulia. I was five, and the Baroness kept chickens. There were chickens everywhere in the formerly grand manse she now had the top floor in, and both my mother and I were sternly warned to watch where we walked because there were eggs everywhere. In fact, there were eggs in my bedroll when I went to sleep, and I woke up the next day, holding in my hands two miraculously unbroken eggs. It seemed to me that over the years this story had become something of a legend among our kin. But my mother, when I asked her about it, said that the Baroness kept little pigs! That, furthermore, I was only three when I went to live with her, and that I was only there for one month. I remembered living there for a year. PIGS! I wasn't about to change anything so dear to me, so I let it slide. A year after the book came out, I was visiting my mother in Washington, D.C., and she said that she felt very sorry that she'd had to leave me with my crazy grandmother and her chickens when I was five years old. BUT MOTHER, I said. PIGS! WHATEVER HAPPENED TO THE PIGS? What pigs? She was annoyed. Denied ever having said anything about pigs. It had been chickens all along.

A strange power this, changing your mother's memory cassette! Her memory just crumbled before the printed page—which may explain in a small way why, in places where history has been falsified by the authorities, people are hard put to remember their true experiences. It's chickens for everybody, whether they like it or not.

My friend Michael Stephens wrote a wonderful memoir called *Season at Coole*. It is composed entirely of fights at the dinner table of his huge New York Irish family. His father never spoke to him after the book was published, and claimed to have never read it. He had been a New York customs official. After his father died, Michael married a Korean girl whose family gave them beautiful old furniture. Thinking to ease the duties on the antiques, Michael told the customs chief at the docks that he was old Mr. Stephens's son. The man looked him over carefully, then asked him: "You're not the one who wrote the book, are you?" "No," said Michael, "that was my brother." "It's a good thing," the boss said, "because we're still looking for the SOB who wrote that book. When we find him we'll break all his bones!" Turns out that old man Stephens had come to the office every morning for the past ten years, read a page of Michael's novel, and made everyone's life miserable the rest of the day.

My own life didn't cause such widespread unhappiness only because my mother wasn't anybody's boss. But she expressed her displeasure emphatically by announcing that she could never share my accomplishment with her friends. "Oh, why," she lamented, "did you have to call it an autobiography? Couldn't you call it a 'novel'?"

It is curious how, in the face of disaster, people suddenly reach for form. At the edge of the abyss they begin to have these formal thoughts. . . . if only the genre had been changed . . . this wouldn't have befallen me. It's like getting religion before dying: one is suddenly beset by alternatives.

Every book needs a proper address. My mother was the one I addressed my first book to because she had been my author until I became one myself. But that isn't why I wrote the book. George Braziller, who published a book of my poetry, glimpsed between the rarefied vistas of my verse certain hints of stories. He suggested I write an autobiography, a suggestion I found absolutely intoxicating. Here I was, twenty-three years old, the possessor of a wealth of experience which had already spawned an equal if not greater quantity of mythicizing anecdotes. I had no ax to grind. I'd changed countries and languages at the age of nineteen, a neat break that could provide a thousand books with rudimentary structure. In addition, I had the numbers: born in 1946, became conscious with the Hungarian revolt in 1956, came to the United States in 1966. Initiatory structures in plain view, natural chapter breaks for the taking. I had already practiced all the anecdotes and revealed their cosmic import to my new American friends, in the process of learning the language. I was learning to view my journey, if not *sub speciae aeternitatis*, than at least as a quest. I was a tragic hero because, most likely, I could never go home again, but I was having a great time on the way. Since I did not speak any English before I came to the United States—with the exception of a single sentence I will tell you shortly—I used my life story to buy my way into my new world. I had no money either. When you're that broke—without language and without money—you are doomed to a kind of choreography, a language of gestures and primal sounds that promise the coming of a story, as soon as some of the details—things like words and food—take their place within the structure. The only thing I had was my story which, I was convinced, was the price of admission to everything. Money, I believed, and still do, is most peoples' substitute for a personal story. The symbols it buys always tell the same story, namely the success story of the prevailing culture back to the culture that spawned it. Money is one's way out of autobiography into the collective myth. The currency of outsiders is their personal story: Here I am. Let me sit by the fire. In return, I'll tell you about these pigs. . . . Of course, not speaking the language intensified the story about to unfold by announcing that it was also a *first* story, a genesis myth. Here I am then, rising from the need to tell my story, gathering language around it as I go, *un pequeno dios* conscious of nothing but its coming into being. And your attention, of course!

The one sentence that I was mighty proud to have put together in English, with the help of my friend Julian in Rome, six months before I came to the US, was:
WHY DON'T YOU KILL YOURSELF?
We tried it out on people around the train station in Rome. A bunch of hustlers and pimps were hanging around the fountain there. We walked up to them:
WHY DON'T YOU KILL YOURSELF? Julian asked.
They had a conference. After some deliberation, one of them pointed us in the direction of the self-service machines inside the station. He thought we'd meant those by "self," places where you could get soft drinks and sandwiches. Since then I've always associated "self" with those "self-service" machines, and think of "self" as a coin-operated contraption.
This primal notion served me well when Mr. Braziller offered

to pay my advance to my life story in monthly installments. I literally constructed my life story in increments spewed out every time he inserted $250.

The Life and Times of an Involuntary Genius was written in the third person (with one chapter, a letter, in the second person singular). I needed this particular distance to view the self under construction. I reserved the first person for oral versions of the story, particularly ones meant to elicit an immediate response: "Hi! I'm Hungarian. Can you spare a dime?"

Ten years after the writing of *Life and Times*, Lawrence Ferlinghetti of City Lights books asked me to write a sequel. He'd read the first one and wondered what had happened afterwards. I was curious myself because what had happened is that, meanwhile, I'd become an American. The sequel, which is not really a sequel at all, is called *In America's Shoes*, and it begins with an address to the Immigration and Naturalization Bureau, an entity I fought a long battle for citizenship with. Instead of addressing myself to my mother I began this book by addressing myself to the state.

In the first chapter the agent in charge of my case is looking through my voluminous file. I see my life passing through the policeman's eyes, arranged in an order alien to me, alphabetized by offenses and suspicions, a life that resembles mine in all but the structure of the narrative. Of course, I tell myself, "file" is an anagram for "life!"

In order to leave the world "my story" rather than "their" story, I proceed to write my autobiography. This time the book is in the first person singular, an emphatic first person at that, because the file is in the third person. The first person now sets up a new distance, not between self and self, but between self and the state. In fact, this book, *In America's Shoes*, is an elaborate identity card.

It was my great luck, coming into America in the late sixties, to encounter several wayward myths ready-made for me, Transylvania being but one of them. Transylvania at the time of my arrival was a growing myth, full of potential, and anybody who bought stock in Dracula then must feel like an investor in early McDonald's. In the past two decades I have seen Halloween overtake Christmas as the nation's greatest holiday, and Dracula become bigger than Jesus Christ, and even John Lennon. Queasy at first about this Hollywood fantasy, I later considered it a gift. The dark stranger who bites blond Anglo-Saxony in her semi-sleep is the outsider, par excellence, the exile who brings history to a halt with his story. His bite ends being in time, it jump-starts eternity, overthrows daytime and the bourgeoise, reinstates aristocracy and difference. And it was a great way to meet girls. I never abandoned the profoundly gloomy existentialist disposition of my rebellious Romanian generation within which I had been raised as a baby dissident destined for great things and prison. No, I just put on a cape to complete the picture. Ionesco, my previous totem, was only a literary Dracula. To be bit by the absurd is every bit as liberating as being bit by an immortal, but why not be bit by both?

The advantages of being a literal exile in a culture obsessed by a myth of it are numerous. The most obvious one was that I was able to gain admittance to a community of my peers with the promise of a story that was, at least in the beginning, only a series of gestures and inarticulate groans. I was able to obtain credit at the bank of the future on the strength of my generic mythical assets.

My mother, who looked for security as well as acceptance, had no active myth to see her on her way. Her generation, in America, was a television-narcotized middle class that had been traumatized by the rebellious younger generation, and was suspicious of foreigners if not downright xenophobic. Her next-door neighbors in Washington, D.C. never smiled, and her attempts at making friends had been rebuffed or perhaps simply lost in the cracks between manners where all the sad foreigners end up. Her story had no one she could properly address it to, which is why she couldn't write her autobiography, no matter how many momentous events had befallen her. She could have addressed it to me, but I'd heard it many times already, and I disagreed most strenuously. My chickens, unless printed, rarely won the day. Her story was by far more tragic, and more typical than mine. She struggled like all energetic immigrants to make a living, and possibly some money. The money was to show the people back home that she'd become a rich and powerful woman. Most of all she wanted friends. She made a living. She didn't make any money. She didn't make many friends. People her own age eluded her because, by and large, they preferred the soap operas they could all enjoy together to the peculiar life story of a single person in broken English. It was not because they lacked compassion but because the same myths that helped me, Dracula and exile, were enemies to them, the myths of their children who caused them nothing but pain. Had my mother become a rich and powerful woman she might have written her autobiography. It would have been addressed to her mother back in the old country, a skeptical soul who never believed that things were different elsewhere. To prove it she lived with chickens—who don't fly far, and can be easily caught and eaten.

Having the assistance of a wayward myth is a special kind of luck, vouchsafed to certain Romanians by Logos Central. Without it, no story can be rightly heard. This is what breaks all those tens of thousands of hearts who imagine that simply because they have had an eventful life there is a reason for writing it down. At times all those cabdrivers who were once former prime ministers, and those heroes of wars no one cares to remember, achieve a kind of epiphany as regards the importance of their lives.

"I wrote this book as a warning: I have lived through terrible things and I have been saved only in order to tell the story. This is my mission: otherwise why did everyone have to die while I went on? And go on, driving this cab which is a vehicle of destiny and a cage for stories. I was neither stronger nor luckier than the rest. Something or Someone kept me here to write this book. But a terrible thing must have happened to this Someone, because no one wants to publish my book. I have no choice but to pay a vanity publisher to publish it: the world will hear my story this way if this is how it has to be. I am going to the bank tomorrow to borrow money against the house. Ah, happy day! The book is published! I will pay the bank back for the book with the money I will make: the world will cry and buy. Or rather buy and cry!"

Days pass, then years. The world isn't buying because the world never sees it. Vanity publishers do not distribute the thousands of sad lives that they publish. They bury them, and that's the final joke. Most people were kept alive not to tell their story but to have their story BURIED. They were kept alive to be made fun of. LIFE IS FUNNY, no doubt about it.

Of all the kinds of literature, autobiographies, no matter how humorous, are the least funny. After all, how much genuine irony can an autobiographer muster? At best he can apply the benign version known as "affectionate irony." Anything stronger would be too strong: one's life, after all, is something one is disinclined to knock, even—or especially—if one wove it out of whole cloth. After all, one has taken the trouble to write it and, if for no other reason, labor must be respected. If one's life seems funny to one the result is more likely to be silence or awkwardness. Life is funny all right, but not the way one was hoping for. Most likely, funny things happen in the course of one's life, and those things, through the insistent refinement of being told over and over become "funny stories" because they amuse listeners over and over, containing as they do, endurable and instructive doses of pain. A collection of these "funny stories" is in truth a terrible thing taken altogether because the life in question is nothing but a series of cover-ups, a horrific giggle stretched over an open wound spanning time. If a life is all "funny stories" the biography itself is the saddest book ever written. The novelist cabdriver who has just banned smoking in his cab finds out that his house is burning. He can add this to the list of instructive experiences for the sake of which he's been kept alive.

In the past two decades, there's been a proliferation of life stories, both autobiographies and thinly disguised autobiographi-cal fiction. The latter, however, for one of those reasons of pub-lishing fashion that are completely mysterious in their transparency, are more in vogue at the moment. "I would like you to write another autobiography," a well-known publisher said to me, "but make it a novel." My mother would have been pleased.

Whence the reluctance? "Whence the reluctance?" I asked him. "Well, to be perfectly frank, you're not famous enough," he said. "This is the time of Iacoccas!" It was. At the American Booksellers' Association meeting that year, every book being pushed was an autobiography by someone who was not a writer. Writers, in other words, if they wanted to live in the same world as the Iacoccas had to hide their lives in novels. Autobiography had suddenly become a form for the rich and famous. There was no call for the outside story. At some point during the time since my last autobiography, time had started flowing backwards. When Andy Warhol said that in the future everyone will be famous for fifteen minutes it sounded funny because time was still flowing forward. Then fifteen minutes became five minutes, then nanosec-onds, and now we can safely say that everyone *was* famous for fifteen minutes at one time or another. Time flows back from the future now, already full of the velocity of a superfluous past which is being divided by several Iacoccas. We are longing to become part of the picture we have already been put out of. The mirrors there, at the junction between past and present, make it appear that there are thousands of Iacoccas. But there are only a few. This is the reason, no doubt, why the retroactive evidence of presence that is the autobiography is such a fiercely awkward phenomenon these days. It is proof of those fifteen minutes, which are now wholly owned by Iacocca Trump.

The future of autobiography is both bright and dim like a TV set. The bright part is that the wealthy dead can now have video screens installed in their tombstones. Push this button, ye stranger going by, and see a life-sized Iacocca appear on screen speaking his life. A coin-operated contraption, this video display offers a choice between fifteen minutes of distilled wisdom from a long life to a full five hours of detailed anecdotes about exactly what it took to bury such a great man.

The dim part is that fewer and fewer people can imagine a life that doesn't look like television. Up to a point, an autobiography would seem to be the exact opposite of television, the stand of the insistently personal against the collectivized story, the small tenant farmer's resistance to the Sovietization of life. But, in fact, we know television families better than our own because they show us everything, while ours, those lumpy shapes on the couch next to us, are completely hidden. How can those strangers be so VISIBLE while we can only watch our dear ones from the narrowing peephole of our own inattentive, inarticulate, amnesiac little selves.

Our own little selves didn't used to be as little as all that. "I contain multitudes," said Walt Whitman, anticipating television by a hundred years, and going on to speak from the platform of that "I" for the multitudes we never really hear except as a background roar, like the sea. Rimbaud's "*je est un autre*" has always been an autobiographer's true challenge, though in my own practice, the *je* est most often *un jeu*.

I once conceived a truly monstrous idea, and went through with it. My third autobiography, covering the ritualistic interval of another ten years, was not going to be either in the first, second or third person singular or plural. I sent out a questionnaire to friends and acquaintances asking them to describe in their own words incidents we experienced together. I asked them to include the story of our meeting, the story of meeting others in our circle, as well as rumors, fantasies and fabrications. There was a special section for composing from the point of view of the subject, "hosting" myself, as it were. I collected some three hundred pages of these testimonials which range from the surreal to the minimal, and began collating them into a single narrative with a view to making a book from the point of view of everyone who has ever admitted knowing me. The "me" under construction here was Nadia Comaneci, the gymnast, the third member of the mythical triumvirate of Ionesco and Dracula. Nadia, the way I saw it, gracefully walked the tightropes of this life, which were actually the seams between the various stories. After being Ionesco and Dracula I wanted to be Nadia. This, I thought, would be the last perspective on my narrative of "self" and, no doubt, my last autobiography. In my first such book I was my own affectionate subject. In the second, I stood up to bad guys and gave them a piece of my mind. In the third, I am no longer speaking. Call me Nadia. Or ABC.

It was a great idea. The only trouble with it was that other peoples' stories—even though they were about "me"—bored me. The stories I had forgotten had something about them that made me see exactly why I had forgotten them. The ones I remembered, I could tell better. It's true moreover that whatever you forget other people remember: it's a nice thing to know in case you need witnesses in court. But amnesia is more important to art than total recall. Amnesia shapes the few remembered or misremembered scenes into whatever you're going to make. The kind of remembering that interests me is anamnesis, which is an intense flashback. Such a flashback is generally devoid of facts because it has room only for feelings. Outfitting these feelings with facts like a grandmother with chicken feathers is a job I like very much. The truth is that I am not all that interested in "myself"—I am only curious to see what kind of person is going to emerge from a certain arrangement of personal stories—which are themselves not "facts" but earlier arrangements—for certain practical uses.

Furthermore, I'm only an inn for the Logos.

My early life story was recently written into a movie script by two well-meaning people. When I went to Los Angeles last week, a producer asked me if I was working on another autobiography.

"As we speak," I told him.

Here is how it starts. I am standing before a distinguished gathering of scholars of autobiographies. I hold forth for various trembling minutes until I realize that I have absolutely no idea how to end. I ramble on and on. The hall empties. I am all alone, rambling on and on. It will be two hundred years before anyone will come back.

Informed of my failure, my mother says: "Didn't I tell you to make it a novel? Oh, why didn't you make it a novel?"

Why indeed?

Not a Pot to Piss In

MY LIFE AS A POT

In giving me a subject as big as the world
the distinguished organizers
showed a lot of faith—
as much faith as mud can have in mud—
Given the vastness and the nature
of the subject prose is wholly inadequate
being both square and utilitarian—
this art I decided will only be served by poetry
which is no simple repository
but rather like a shapely pot itself a wholly
surprising recasting of the matter—
Much like humans beings themselves, of course,
who were fashioned by god
to store his thoughts in.
God's scattered thoughts were a constant source
of confusion to him
until he conceived of two faithful mugs
that would be a perfect metaphor for his job
which was filling the emptiness.
On the other hand god may have just been playing
and had no need of either metaphors or storage
or frames for his thoughts—
Metaphors and storage may have been the problem
of his playthings—
his playthings having come into being
experienced an anxiety of definition:

what are we and what are we for, they cried,
soon after being shaped,
and hearing no answer, provided themselves
with metaphors, raison d'etres and other uses.
I like to think that ontological anxiety is the exclusive
property of the created, that the maker has none.
And of course I may be wrong.
We do seem to be made by anxious gods sometimes.

When I was young and didn't have a pot to piss in
I thought a lot about god.
In my cups often my cup overfloweth with god
and I was full of inspiration.
Human life from chamber pot to funeral urn
is a ceaseless pouring from one vessel into another,
I reasoned, so *enivrez-vous* as
Baudelaire said, and when I was perfectly drunk
I was in paradise like a happy jug.

For most of the time in paradise
the primero living pots
had no need of other pots
because rivers flowed directly
into their mouths and whenever they looked up
something delicious and ripe fell for them to eat—
they were perfect self-referential pots
required only to believe in their own self-replenishing
   sufficiency and in the skill of the demiurge—
but then something got into them
   —probably the unsettling thought that they were a metaphor—
and they tried to make pots on the sly while god was sleeping—
they snuck into the shed and started fooling around with his
   cosmic wheel—
and god smashed them to the earth and they were broken into
   shards—
whose history we never stop trying to piece together

out of the shards we ourselves have left behind—
millions of shards because since the Fall
we've had to ceaselessly keep
making pots to store our food, eat and drink from,
     and write our stories on.

But this god didn't stop there.
He forbade the making of idols as well
and outlawed any object that wasn't plain and functional
such as fat goats, nard boxes, seductive vials and dolls—
so that there was no more arguing with this god
about ceramic art—
and all ceramicists henceforth became pagans.
And as for humans themselves
he imprisoned them forever
in their original forms
so that we are all djinns and djinnies in the jugs
of our flesh waiting for death to let us out.
When I was young I thought a lot about history
and about women
and when my cup overflowed
I often conversed with the djinnie in the jug
& she obliged me with a parade of vessels of eros
from the mysteries of all religions
from Semiramis to Delphi
a profusion of Lilliths and Venuses
whose cornucopic flow made me giddy & amorous.
It was a wholly different creation I saw under their spell.
In this one after god fashioned
woman from the mud
he had just enough left over to make her a pet.
So he made her a boy poet.

Not so—an older & wiser drinkard told me.
After god made man and woman
he blew life—or faith—into the man

and then tired went to put more fire into his breath
leaving the dog in charge of the urn that was
going to be woman
and the devil came up and asked the dog:
Please dog please can I play with this form?
I'll give you a fur coat if you let me play with this form.
OK, said the dog, and the devil played with the form
and put ninety moods in her.
When god came back he was mad:
Because you let the devil play with my form, dog,
you will wear your coat forever even in summer.
And that was one hot dog from then on.

Well, then, I told the older drinkard,
I propose to you that if god was the first potter
the devil was the first artist
and the dog the first buyer, admirer, gawker and fool.
And as for woman and her moods
they continue to produce the metaphors
as well as the actual objects
we slog through history with,
objects which festoon even the bible like a museum
from the wedding at Caana to the platter holding John's head,
inspite of god's express command against playing with mud
    or fire or yourself—
a Pandora's box full of dishes, cups, jugs, pitchers and urns
on which are carved the bodies & faces of people past & present
    whose fingers shaped them, and left their mark—
And this bounty, this cornucopia, this generative
    formal imagination is the reason why we eventually survived,
spilling out of the disappointment of losing paradise into an
    eros of our own celebrated by daily ware
    as well as by ceremonial clay—

And of course by now it was much later
not only in history but in the night

and I would have given all the empty cups
piled between us on the table like a tomb
for a girl or woman with a living womb.

When I got home I fumbled with the key
in the moonlight that barely lit the ancient keyhole
of our Saxon house in Transylvania.
Shining from the glass case which mother kept
under a different lock and key
were seven plates from mother's village
in the mountains, and a cheap porcelain Napoleon
she had picked up at some Austrian fair.
The patterns on the dishes could also be found
in the embroidery of certain dresses at the back
of her closet which stood there mysteriously alert.
About the plates I knew only that they were meant
for special days that had not yet arrived
in my lifetime. A wedding perhaps. Mine? Hers?
A feast so grand the whole apartment block would come.
All our neighbors, former peasants mostly, had been
forced by misery and decrees to move into the city,
and they all displayed in cases similar to ours
the plates of their villages, mysterious discs inscribed
with the signs of their particularity, the lost
co-ordinates of lives that had once been round and cosmic
and revolved like saucers about the saucers and the plates
of their specific differences. They were maps these plates
of lives once lived in cyclical ease, maps of a handmade world
that knew the wherefores of its food and celebrated
its making and its transformation in the proper ware.
These dishes waited for their weddings now
in cement cubicles hived about the steel industries
of our town. One day, I told myself, you'll get
to set them all in their full splendour on the tables
covered with handmade lace and linens. It will be
the wedding of the sun with the moon, and all the stars

will stand there burning patterns as they eat.
But no such day. My mother had by now relegated
these dishes to the status of display, and she had
for the most part forgotten their provenance, and their
meaning. She placed them on the same plane as her cheap
Napoleon, and was mighty ticked that morning when
she found him smashed into a hundred bits, even his hand
which he kept so carefully in his coat. It appears
that in my drunken glory I had climbed up on the case
and holding him in my hand I had made a speech about
the loss of our selves and our roots in jumbled signs
and when I was done I hurled him to the floor.
That much for the glory of reflected lore.

The Saxons who founded Hermannstadt were craftsmen.
The Bruckenthal Museum was full of ceramics & terrors,
    Laocoon was forever strangled by faiance snakes
    & there were snakes curled on plates & bemused fish
    stretching their scales between centuries from Holland
        to Transylvania, and monsters perched above toureens
    who had travelled from Vienna after devouring their diners,
    & scenes of China and Japan patiently waiting for their victims
        to be done eating
        & Greek oil jars in which thieves had slowly dissolved—
    & it was no safer outside the museum where Ilse
the fraulein who took care of me when mother worked
took me to her Black Forest house with the ceramic
German stove for cooking children in the middle of her
        bedroom—When I was asleep she put two hot bricks
        at my feet & roasted me as her porcelain dolls shrieked—
In those days under every bed
was an enormous chamber pot held down by angels
in which lived a fin-de-siecle monster filled with children's
    brains—And all these things were glazed & shiny & full of
    history.

In a country where there weren't many things
where the material world was both thin & threadbare—
you could easily see the light shining through it—
we loved & feared our chamber pots and stoves fiercely
even as we could not remember what was written on them.
But things were certainly written on them
and those few of us who knew how to read read them
without surcease. Ilse, for instance, read Gothic script
to me in the Bruckenthal, intoning Mittel Deutsch like a Latin
    mass—
And now & then in the chiaro-oscuro of the Bruckenthal which was
    saving money on lights I would encounter an old scholar
    named Ferenc Pasperger who always made notes & wore a coat
    so shiny & so thin you could see his yellow parchment skin
    underneath. One afternoon he bid me put my ear to the bulge
    of a pot that was quite a bit taller than me
    & had grooves on its fat belly. "Listen!" he said. I listened.
I heard something like a far-off sea something I'd heard before
    in seashells. I told him so. "No, listen deeper!," he said,
    and as I did it seemed to me that I heard voices talking,
    shouting, laughing at some great distance, behind a wall.
I heard children. "That's it! That's it!," said Ferenc, his bony
    forehead close to mine. "Those are," he said, "the voices
    of the people who made this pot, and you can hear their
    children talking, and whoever was around just then."
It was true. I listened most of that afternoon and heard people
    long dead conversing in the pot.
Ferenc thought that the grooves were like grooves on a record
    and that the makers of pots used their tools to record
    their worlds, and that we could hear them if we listened.
And that fired my imagination & I thought that I could listen
    to Socrates, for instance, if only I found the right pot
    because he hung out in the market around the pot makers
    & the mob, or to anyone for that matter, and that I could
    pick up secrets whispered within range of the turning stylus:

hints of hidden treasure, plots to kill, the mumbled seeds
of conversation that became Gilgamesh, or Don Quixote or
The Last Testament of Francois Villon—
And ever since then I've been listening. I put my ear to the old
    pots and hear the vanished people gab. And sometimes I pick
    them up, the great and the not so great dead I steal
    my verses from—

Hidden on dishes, pots and sculptures in plain sight
is our history and our peculiar rhythms—

I also found a little later—
I was growing up fast in those days—
that in the old cemetery
among the amputated angels and the listing urns
were ideal places to hide with a girl.
I hid there with Aurelia.
One summer afternoon she and I lay on the bodies
of two knights carved with their arms crossed
on their tombstones
who made a low sorrowful moan of long gone love
until we tumbled between them and there on the broken
debris we commenced the old dance.
Many times the startled angels sighed and fell
off their pedestals while the urns tipped as our hot
fire passed through them.
And then it rained & you could hear the dead
straining to leave the squishy slimy squeaky mud
and to burst their binds of crumbling stone
as we continued
working the clay and shards with our bodies
until it was time to go home and catch hell—
those days were full of cracked & babbling ceramics,
urns, jugs & broken pillars to hide behind—
we were like statues or dolls ourselves:

still when the adults were watching
& animated & full of an insane music when they were not.

Having decided to be a poet for reasons having to do
partly with all the whispering text about me
and partly because I was full like a jug with
all the milk of my adolescence
I began putting words on paper
though only incidentally on paper—
I would have liked to write on clay tablets.
Failing that I would
have liked to inscribe the bowls
we slurped our gruel from so that in getting to the bottom
the startled glutton would be confronted suddenly
with his own mortality: "He who made this bowl
salutes you. From now on you are his. Obey his oracle,
you greedy dog!" Or: "You've gotten to the bottom. From
here on out only the journey matters."
In the fifties Communism achieved a Zen-like simplicity.
It was every man and his bowl.
And it was every woman and her single potato
or, on holidays, a bone.
Books were even scarcer.
The only things to eat or to read were signs from the past.
And these were written on dishes kept under lock and key.
And on small things that fell on us in the cemetery
from the toppled funeraria: old coins, spiders, withered hearts,
    dried livers and coarse spiny flowers.

Consequently, our imaginations were free to spin.
We spun imaginary beings which
unlike the flesh ones are always spun not born.
We were all mind potters turning the wheels of our
blooming flesh into a void made cold by ideology.
And it was a muddy world too because as soon

as you left the dimly lit city with her cracked pavements
and her crackling, sighing and swaying cemetery
you were back in the stew-thick dark of peasant villages
yoked to skinny nags and sluggish oxen
whose job was not to pull these villages anywhere
into, let's say, the 20th century
but to keep them anchored rather
to the Carpathian mountains—
They groaned there at the heart
of dismembered feudal estates,
shadowed by monasteries and castles perched on crags—
in one of these at Arges
a young girl had been built alive into the wall
so that the wall would stand—
and in another Countess Bathory drank
the blood of 650 virgin girls
in order to keep her youth—
and ghosts were still drinking from stone cups
a substance that could have been time itself—
they did not care about communism
they did not anticipate capitalism
they looked rather into a farther past
for that single object, the Grail, and its connection
to god, or some god, or some essential magic.

It can be argued of course that the Grail was itself
capitalism, that its function was to transform the creative
blood or sweat of the divine into the multitude
of objects that fill the world now. The alchemists'
alembics, grinders, mortars, pestles and jars, moved
steadily toward the generative heart of matter where
the pure transformative operation percolated in its sealed
container. Not far from us, in Prague, a rabbi
made a man of clay called a Golem and gave him life
by writing the name of god on his forehead, and when

this lyric statuette began behaving badly the rabbi
did to him what god did to us. He erased the word
and the creature crumbled.

Communism was a golem by the mid-sixties.
It awaited only the hand to erase the word.
God had pretty much been done away with by then
both in the East and the West.
After a time the unsettled creation
that had issued from the lord's kilns
came to the rather
chilling conclusion
that only the murder of god could
restore it to paradise. This conclusion, I must add, was
chilling but inevitable, given the magnitude of our loss
and the grudge we carried ever since we were hurled
like cheap Napoleons from our golden-pot selves into
the muck of history,
the story of which we have scratched into every
available surface
and would have continued to do so to this day
had history not ended & the electronic media
taken its place.
But that's another story.
In the intervening centuries
between the Fall & the deicide
we elaborated our revenge—
by the middle of the 19th we had it—
we did to god what he did to us—
we pulled god out of the heavens
and when he fell he too broke into a thousand shards—
that's why there are so many god-struck people now.
This was but simple justice though it is nice that we observed
    the forms
and had Nietzsche sign the official death certificate.
These god-struck people walking about with god-shards

imbedded in their brains
amble about in large numbers
   while the larger shards
float above their heads and are called flying saucers
   and in this form are seen daily by millions
in the sky and the popular press—
   Though it could also be the case
that some of these saucers were made by ceramicists
   in California & loosened upon the rest of us.
                    (You know who you are!)

The 19th century happened for me around my 19th year.

It is not coincidental that both the 19th century
   and my 19th year
were the sites of an overwhelming profusion of dishes,
pots and soup toureens, broken gravestone angels,
leaf-stuffed gargoyles trying to cough them out,
clay-born worlds
that multiplied in panic and in response
to chimney stacks and factories—
the Victorian world was making a last stand for the handmade
craft in the kitchens and the boudoirs
which gave birth to Freud—
while out of the smoking chimneys of mass-production
Karl Marx was born—
and as for me I was considering marrying Aurelia the girl
from my hometown whose dowry
consisted of one hundred plates
displaying Minoan-like fertility charms
ancient designs that came from Minos via Illyria to Dacia Felix
two marble jars that looked Cretan,
a serpentine goblet that could have been used in Babylonia,
and two hundred black bowls with a red glaze
matched by two hundred cups
with a snake beneath each handle—

an incredible wealth that had come unbroken
through her mountain-folk who had traded
sheep for centuries in the Black Sea-Mediterranean world
where eventually the amphoras of Greece, Rome and Byzantium
encountered the spice jars, oil jugs and wine goblets of the
    Orient, including those huge Arabian Nights pots where Ali
    Baba and the forty thieves hid—

even as the rest of her mother's culture lay in shards
all about her—
her mother worked in a textile factory.
In the end it was all for the best.
We would not have gotten along
and all those dishes would have doubtlessly
broken on the shoals of our stormy relationship.

I took my writing tablets elsewhere then—
to the West
to a world of happy plastic
a universe of melmac
nylon, vinyl lounge chairs,
naugah interiors and lava lamps
where the products of ersatz Freud
reclined sipping chemicals
through plastic straws
from tall mass-produced goblets.
This was the Dow Country
the country of Dow Chemical and napalm.

Thank god for the hippies.
And for Latin America.
In potter sheds inside a secret nation
the children of the plastic people
were making another world
out of clay.
In California I lived with several potters

who made self-refilling coffee mugs, bottomless
  bean pots, self-cleaning ashtrays & vanishing tea cups
that imparted to the tea-drinkers an uncanny Japanese-style
  kind of peace that after surpassing all understanding
  led to some fabulous Kabuki-like theatre & sex.
And when my friends talked about their pots it always sounded
  to me as if they were talking about sex:
  they said wide shoulders, thickened mouth rim, cobalt
    blue under the glaze, long neck, undulating rim, deeply
    recessed, high flaring foot, and once there was
    buff stoneware covered with a white slip. That one
    really got me.
And I could see how one could fall in love with a pot as if it
  were a person & many of my friends
were in fact in love with pots who were a lot less damaged
  than the human fauna that spinned about the place.
And my wife Alice had a dream about a village clustered around
  a pyramid atop which wise elders sat smoking and chatting
and she spent the next year making it: a multitude of villagers
  engaged in tasks about the wells and the fields, women cooking
  children dancing in a circle, people staring out the windows
  & in the middle of it was the pyramid and the elders &
  she called this The Clay People's Republic &
  when she finished it I had a dream that all the people
  who ever lived were now here again made out of clay
  awaiting only a signal to start going about their business
  & I woke up wondering how we would all fit
  on the same earth which is getting smaller as I speak—
In Mexico just across the way
a myriad of gods, goddesses and fetishes
also came out of the ground
and out of kilns
in a jumble of archeology & modernity
pre-columbian past below
insurgent new muralista colors above.
I saw a terra-cotta dog with a human mask

made in Colima
a native hairless dog
and a clay model of an Aztec ball court
with eager spectators
and countless males and females holding
things that looked like rockets—
and clay masks
and priests, shamans, nobles and peasants,
whole worlds, friendly and unfriendly,
representing the seen and the unseen—

but most of all I saw myself
seated at a stall in a plaza of the New World
writing letters for hire for illiterate lovers
while underneath my papers there was a stone tablet
on which the writing I did on paper
inscribed itself simultaneously in a cuneiform-type language
that only few could read.
And I became quite the fetishist as you can see.
And in 1989 communism collapsed,
the word gone from its forehead.
The borders of the empires blurred.
The clays across official borders
became visible, an intermingling
that could be fertile & rich.
But simultaneously the pots of small nations
rose from their buried hovels full
of the unsettled honey of a thousand lost wars.
These drums of tightly packed sentiment & hate
are now being carried on the shoulders of hungry mobs
who want them opened, worshipped and divined.
How we break them open without destroying their beauty
or mocking their pain
is the challenge of our art—

My friends, potters digging up the earth

leaving holes in it until the whole mass of it
becomes artifact or art
you must divine the vectors of its new order—
that's the price for not keeping still in paradise.

After words ceramics are the most legible writing
and words themselves are written mostly upon the dishes
to which I keep my ear,
and what they say is,
it's a long story of mud & of hands
and the hands that fashion the mud refashion the world—
when little hands play in the clay
they make monsters and warriors who pummel each other
who have names & things to say to each other
and twirling ballerinas and princesses who also
have names & things to say to each other
& in play all return to childhood

even self-intoxicated adolescents in their cups
who think a lot about god

that poor god without a pot to piss in
whose shards are now everywhere to be found

Whose Worlds Are These?

IN JUNE 1967 THE CANDYMAN BURST THROUGH the door of my pad on Avenue C in New York's Lower East Side. He always burst through the door because that was his style. He could barely contain himself. He dropped his mirrored Peruvian bag on the kitchen table and exclaimed: "Just for you! Czech acid!" The Candyman always had some kind of acid. That month I had already sampled Windowpane and Sunshine. I didn't know if my system could handle another extended flight to the far reaches. But this Czech acid *was* different. For one thing, it revealed to me that the entire molecular and sub-molecular structure of the universe was in fact composed of tiny sickles and hammers. Billions and billions of tiny sickles and hammers shimmered in the beauteous symmetry of the material world. I always thought of this particular "commie trip" as a rather private experience brought about by my having been born and raised in Communist Romania where sickles and hammers were ubiquitous and unavoidable. I did not doubt that I had seen them but I did doubt whether there was such a thing as Czech acid for the simple reason that Czechoslovakia, like Romania, was a monochromatic world. Acid would have brought about the collapse of communism just as it was bringing about the collapse of a certain kind of dour-faced simpleminded America. And at that time, it didn't look like communism was anywhere near collapse. Well, I was wrong.

Reading *Acid Dreams: The C.I.A., the Sixties and Beyond*, by Martin A. Lee and Bruce Shlain, I found, on page 115, that: "In September 1965 Michael Hollingshead returned to his native London armed with hundreds of copies of the updated *Book of the Dead* and five thousand doses of LSD (which he procured from Czech government laboratories in Prague)." Well, I'll be switched. Communism did collapse, though not right then, and acid *did* have quite a bit to do with it. Charter 77, the Czech human rights organization, was founded by Vaclav Havel in defense of the Plastic People of the Universe, a psychedelic band inspired by the Velvet Underground. Havel himself was in New York in 1968 listening to the Velvet and dreaming, no doubt, of a way out of Cold War ideology.

This tiny revelation is but a small parenthetical remark in a story full of surprises, many of which are profoundly unsettling. The drug that connected so many of us to the organic mystery of a vastly alive universe turns out to have been, at least in the beginning, a secret CIA project to find a "truth serum." It's scary to think that CIA spooks have used LSD with electroshock and torture in order to get information out of their prisoners. it's scarier that they have used it themselves to little positive effect. (Or perhaps not.) It's ironic and still scary to think that the CIA tried to control the LSD experiment to the very point where hundreds of thousands were turning on in the heydays of the sixties. Neither the ironies nor the chilling implications stop here. There was a complex tissue of connections between secret government agencies and the academic world, on the one hand, and between the utopian hopes of a generation and the machinations of those same agencies, on the other. The most paranoid and outlandish theories of the sixties seem insufficiently paranoid.

Nonetheless, the vibrant collective aura of the times, despite the CIA and Army Intelligence, managed to change America forever. The undeniably metaphysical window that LSD opened for so many of us may have unwittingly been opened by those whose interests lay in keeping it shut. It may well be that, seeing their mistake, they have been endeavoring to close it ever since. But the fact is that the brilliant glimpse of a living cosmos did pour through for a while and it resulted in an unprecedented vision of a different world. One could debate forever the question of how much of what the drug did for us was contingent on the peculiar conditions of that time. The opening was real.

The importance of LSD goes beyond nostalgia. The effect of the drug on the psychology, sociology and politics of the sixties has created the mythos and poetry that now permeate almost every aspect of high and low American culture. Capital C Conspiracy was part of the story but for those, like myself, who believe that conspiracy and control are games that vanish once one ceases to believe in them, the story goes on. To history buffs, this is merely fascinating history. For some of us it's an ongoing thriller about the great mystery of how we, of a certain generation, got to be who we are.

Platonism
or Why the World's Fucked Up

ALL MY RELATIONSHIPS ARE PLATONIC. THEY GET
that way right after sex. Platonism was invented, I'm sure, in that
state known as *post coitum anima triste* or, in American, after
shtooping the soul sags. In that state of soul-sag the infinite
sadness of one's animal limitations make for a dream state out of
which Plato is born, every time. Plato, if you recall, thought that
we human critters are only shadows, pale imitations of an ideal
that is eternal and unachievable and that probably happened a
long time ago, in the past, long before we assumed the mortal
coils. People of the Platonic persuasion do not put much stock in
our actions here in this vale of flesh tears. Consequently, some of
them do not even bother with the flesh. They prefer to dwell in
the realms of fleeting thought and obscure meta-intuitive sorrow.
They can't wait to get out of their bodies.

I am not, alas, of that school. If I see a body I want to touch
it. Smell it. Watch it. Since I am hopelessly heterosexual (not for
lack of trying!), I am attracted mostly to the female form toward
which I make many friendly gestures. I have a great many friends,
male and female. The quality of these friendships depends not on
any platonic ideal but in the substance of our interchanges, most
of which are physical and happen right here in this world. I touch
my male friends too, though not sexually. I touch them on the
shoulders, I slap them on their backs, I pump their hands, we slap
five, we shadowbox. I grew up in Romania, in Europe, where
friends of the same sex were not afraid to hold hands in school
or get drunk and sway with their arms about each other. Men in

America don't get to do that for fear of being thought queer, and it's a shame and a pity. With my women friends, it's a different story. I touch them in friendly ways too, but tenderly, with more curiosity. I never posit any platonism between us and if encouraged I will drag them to bed without any qualms. If not encouraged, then, of course, I'll go platonic. Sigh. It's happened. But here is the thing: physical intimacy or possible intimacy is only a device for opening the floodgates to what really matters: words. What I want from my friends, male or female, are words. Great torrents of conversation, ramblings, monologues, infinite confidences, stories, anecdotes, confessions. I know that there are silent friendships out there just like there are platonic ones. I don't hold to those. I like my friendships warm, fleshy, verbal, sensual, sensorial and adventurous. Plato was a crank—and he hated women.

II Television & War

"If it's working, it's already obsolete!"—that is the paradox of the West, which we haven't sufficiently pondered, and which became Lord Mountbatten's motto during the last war, when he directed British weaponry research.
PAUL VIRILIO

Like the Party, whose unstated rules no person can follow rigidly enough, TV demands that its extruded viewers struggle to embody an ideal too cool and imprecise for human emulation.
MARK CRISPIN MILLER

Happiness of the Mass-Media Man (with asides on Death)

WE WERE TALKING ABOUT TV OVER DRINKS AT the Napoleon House and someone observed how pathetic it was that four intelligent people would spend so much time talking about TV in a place like the Napoleon House, which features dimness, classical music, dreamy brews and interesting people. But this sort of thing is everywhere these days: no matter how interesting, intelligent, well-educated or good-looking the people conversing are they will all eventually end up talking about either TV or movies.

One of us ventured an explanation: "TV sets our standards of normalcy *and* our standards of happiness. So we tune in to see just how deviant we are and how far from achieving the happiness of someone in a TV commercial who just got a Ford van."

I wondered out loud if happiness had changed any since, say, a decade ago when people didn't have computers in their pockets.

I posed myself the same question later after I poured a Jim Beam and turned on the Boob Tube. It was a hard question because it required rising briefly above the unconscious bath of the mass media in whose troubled waters I and my fellow citizens lead our everyday lives, in order to watch TV *critically*, something I find impossible. TV bypasses my mind entirely. Its beams lodge in a diffuse but dense pattern between the crotch and the solar plexus. I have no trouble talking about food while eating or about sex while having it: those are enhancements. But talking (or thinking) about TV while watching it is not like that, it's more like espousing a rival religion sotto voce while the priest preaches the official creed loudly.

Was there anything new in the way we are sold happiness these days, something that wasn't there in, let's say, the fifties, the sixties, the seventies or the eighties? I watched intently for three minutes. I didn't know how long I could survive in the pure air of detachment outside the set but I tried, I really did.

Of course, it would have been a heck of a lot easier to ask the real question: what's new in *un*happiness? I could have answered that because I'm an earthling living in the United States of America at the end of the twentieth century, and things, no matter what TV tells you, have been getting worse. And part of the reason why they have gotten worse is because TV tells us what happiness is.

Happiness according to my TV was a state of exaltation without content(ment), made up entirely of orgasmic moments, a never-ending sequence of explosions that even (an endlessly deferred) death may not cure. One hundred dogs were kneeling before a doughnut shop. They had seen god. A woman was making headache circles around her head. Her halos hurt. But fear not: Advil, an anti-saint, galloped forth to knock those halos off. There was good news for the thirty billion yeast sufferers: a new method to make bread and feed the masses was being patented. A jukebox dropped in on a couple and destroyed their house.

What was going to happen to all these people after they'd seen god, knocked off their halos, fed the masses and lost their homes? It was a failure of the advertising on my TV that it did not deal with the afterlife of the people in the commercials. It dawned on me as I sat there that advertising was still in its infancy, that it had not yet tackled the most lucrative domain of all, it had not yet opened up the vast market of death. In spite of the otherworldliness of the events depicted in the exemplary hyperspace of ads the subjects were still mucking about the narrow confines of human life.

"I want advertising to show me what happens after death," I said to no one in particular. "It is the only imaginative force capable of picturing the afterlife. Which is all montage." (When you talk to yourself like this—with the TV set blaring—make sure no one except the readers of *Organica* overhear you.)

Ads have conquered all the other primal areas, especially sex and food. But why not death? In looking at the mind-boggling revenue potential of death, I was surprised that advertisers hadn't been able to get past peddling hospital rooms and coffins. They hadn't been able, in other words, to conquer the territory now mined by televangelists, who are slick but old-fashioned salesmen of the other world.

There had to be a secret here. No happiness is complete without a satisfying afterlife. Advertising holds the mirage of happiness before us at a seemingly reachable distance. In reality, there is no closing the gap. It moves out of reach whenever we come closer. In the gap there reigns an increasing tension and a constant low-grade anxiety that can only be assuaged by *buying*. The material world has only one purpose: to reproduce in order to be con-sumed. That is why every version of happiness on television refers to reproduction in one way or another, using sex just the way nature uses sex: to trick one into reproducing. "I hate copulation and mirrors," said the Argentine poet Borges, "because they both multiply people." In the mirror-game of advertising, the object is the multiplication of things to buy. TV creates desire by its depic-tions of possible happiness, but it's a desire that can never be satisfied. It is true that the dead do not desire things, which makes them terrible consumers, but the living desire an affluent afterlife. The explanation may be that there aren't enough afterlife products yet. The wing-and-halo factories haven't yet risen from the hokey into the everyday eternity. No one yet knows that the dead need jukeboxes, dancing shoes, BBQ guards, agony amplifiers . . . all the things of this world plus some.

In light of its basic terrestrial mission to the living there was really nothing new about advertising's hyping of material happi-ness on my TV, but the ads were better than the last time I remembered watching them. Their greatest success seemed to be in the area of getting rid of certain sentimental notions that still held some of us back, notions like the traditional family, concern for other life-forms, concern for other human beings, and nature. There was a great perceptive gulf, for instance, between the seventies ideal of happiness bodied in the injunction DON'T FOOL WITH MOTHER NATURE and the nineties incitement to JUST DO IT. If the people of the seventies could be suspected of harboring somewhere in their atrophied liberal hearts a notion of happiness that involved something bigger than their immediate selves, that was completely gone in the nineties. Mother Earth was a force to be reckoned with then, a force that urged some restraint in order to achieve contentment. But now we wouldn't let anything and anybody stand in our way, not even Mother Earth. Just Do It.

Mother Earth has been going the way of all mothers in American life as well as on American TV. She has become a single breadwinner with a fierce need for easy-listening music and sexual fantasy, all but unattainable amid the landscapes of dirty laundry she must traverse and the children she somehow must turn over to the army in reasonably good shape. Traditional mothers with long pasta-stirring spoons have all but vanished from television to be replaced by microwave moms on their way out the door. Occasionally, harried young housewives tortured by mountains of children's dirty socks show up between soap opera episodes high on coffee. Most often, however, they are to be found around the office watercooler discussing feminine hygiene. More and more, mothers and daughters are indistinguishable age-wise. The mother's hands are younger than the daughter's, and it is not even certain that the mother knows the best feminine protection. The daughter is usually up on the newer things which she has learned from, you guessed it, television. Nor are things better between mothers and sons. Time was when mother, upon seeing a hole in one of her boy's garments, would patch it right up. But now holes are in, made by machines, and her job is to buy the holey pants and to stay out of the picture.

Even more invisible than mothers are fathers. In the nineties father doesn't only not know best, he doesn't know *anything*. He doesn't know where he is (unless he's in his car) and he doesn't dispense any advice (nobody's listening). He's all but nonexistent. He's rarely fixing things around the house because he lives in a singles' apartment building now where everything is fine not only because "GE brings good things to life" but because he and his buddies can drink Lite beer until the cows come home. He's never tired of his buddies, or tired period, because the Eveready batteries that power his world can keep going forever and past that, traversing different worlds and different commercials just like *the life force itself*, the vital current.

The truth is, the family, as seen on TV commercials, is dead. It has been replaced by one's peer group, mostly same-sex gangs, that lead a boisterous indoor life in anonymous mall-cities where everything in the world is for sale close at hand. These gangs live segregated by age-group (and often by sex) in separate ghettos in mall-America. Young folks are in the sports and fern bars, old folks are in security areas. The only nature allowed into these suburban enclosures is the fantasy of nature occasioned by a new car. This car, fast and powerful, can lead one directly to an idyllic spot in nature, a spot that, however, has nothing to do with nature itself but serves only as a setting for sex with one of the beautiful members of the opposite-sex gang.

The picture of the late twentieth-century American ideal of happiness as seen on my TV consisted of frantic indoor activity by segregated consumer gangs. In fact, happiness has been redefined to resemble TV commercials (which formerly aimed to resemble an *existing* ideal). TV happiness was not a peaceful activity: it manifested in concentrated bursts that took the form of elation, joy, ecstasy and other abnormal manifestations. According to the world my TV made for me, sober human beings could not conceivably be happy. So I poured another bourbon, my fifth.

We all, with few exceptions, live on TV now. The exceptions belong to that race of childlike angelic beings we put in "special" schools. Here in the South where we sometimes take personal care of our peculiar "grown-ups" you may see one of these moon-faced children of light now and then, mopping diligently the corner of the mom-and-pop restaurant under the blaring TV set that does not in the least touch his blessed awareness. Not so the customers who miss their mouth with the lima bean soupspoon while watching a tight-jeaned nymph slide across the dream landscape that could be—and probably is—their own (absent) mind. Let's face it, only an idiot can be happy in today's TV-conditioned world. Touched by Calvin Klein obsessions, tragic nymphs tremble on their Lorelei rocks with nostalgia for fascism. The roommate freshener sweeps the room for alien organisms. Faces on fingers shake their heads. They can't believe it's not butter.

Where does this leave contentment, that ingredient deemed necessary by all cultures for any true happiness? It is conceivable that somewhere in a deep pocket of forgotten countryside there are people content with who they are, the place where they live and how much money they make. But I doubt if these people will be content for very long if their piece of paradise includes a TV set. The images of happiness that radiate from the box are without contentment; they induce only the discord that leads to the attempt to quell it by buying. Not in a million years will any reasonably content person be as perfectly content as the people on TV. No matter how happy one happens to be at the moment one can never be as happy as the woman who wears a deodorant gentle enough for a woman but strong enough for a man. Contentment, which was once the (rare) property of (rare) humans has now become the exclusive attribute of people in commercials.

There is a simple explanation for this: we never *watch* ourselves being happy so we never know just how happy we *look*. We may *be* happy but if not we don't look it; at least part of this happiness is bogus because this is an image-based society. Pardon me, you have something at the corner of your mouth. . . . drool! Wipe your mouth, put your head down, and keep mopping. You are clearly an idiot.

The happy ones on TV, unlike us, are two-dimensional. Their purpose is to sow strife, discontent and revolution among us, the living. (If we are still!) If you are married TV makes you wish that you were single. If you are single TV makes you want to be part of that merry gang of your Lite-beer drinking peer group. If you are part of that merry gang, it makes you wish that you were the leader of it. If you are the leader of it, you don't have a good enough car. If you have a good enough car, you'll need a good enough woman (man). If you've got one of those you'll need a better deodorant. If you smell good enough to be a couple you'll need better medicine for your headaches. If you entertain you'll need better class than your neighbors and have the coffee that'll prove it. And when at long last you lie on your happy marital bed having survived the insufficiencies of youth, same-sex bonding and the pitfalls of body image and body odor, you lie awake because you are sexually dysfunctional and need a therapist, an insurance agent, an accident lawyer, Rogaine for your hair, a good, caring hospital and a mental institution to put your children in. And if you succeed at all this, don't be too cocky: you're still fat.

The alien who fell to earth in the movie *The Man Who Fell to Earth*, was an obsessive TV watcher. He was looking for cues to something that would help him become one of us. He could recite thousand of lines from old movies befitting every situation but something kept eluding him. He couldn't keep up with the incredibly fluid, changing picture of TV beings. Self-definition under the steady downpour of new ideas of self was more difficult than his tragic journey through space. It was a good thing that he was an alien, which is to say that he was alienated to start with.

It's not so easy for the rest of us. The ideals of consumer culture have made aliens out of all of us. We have little choice but to try keeping up with the happiness eternally promised by the mirage box, a process that makes us stranger than ever to ourselves and to our kind. We have little choice, of course, except turning off the box, but it might be too late for that. Any such attempt and *it* will turn *us* off first.

The fact is, TV has already turned us off. All my speculations about the commercial and advertising potential of death is pointless because TV has not already entered that market but it deals in nothing but. The only living people are those in ads. They sell to the dead. That's us. Have another bourbon.

Ed McMahon:
The Sweepstakes of Fat

THEY ARE UNLOADING BAGS OF MONEY ON THE lawn next door. Grotesque suburbanites in oversized clothes are flinging cash in the air. The cash is actually fat—burning. The armored truck guards are watching sternly so that the unlucky neighbors watching over the fence—the Stringbeans—will not vault over and rip the happiness from the Fatsos. Filling the horizon is the face of God, Ed. Ed is fat—and because he is fat he makes it possible for fat Americans to be happy. Santa Claus is fat. Most Americans are fat. Therefore most Americans are Santa. But there can only be one Santa because this is a representative democracy—so all the fatsos have voted for Ed Santa. He is the Grand Santa. He is America. He is fat.

Where did Ed grow fat? Ed grew fat in the shadow of Johnny. Johnny is not fat because Johnny drinks scotch and is a generic millionaire. Johnny is a little rich boy who kicks Ed. Ed is Johnny's sidekick, a beer drinker, a grunt. But he is also a dad. Women like Johnny. Men like Ed. Johnny likes himself. Ed likes money, beer and fat. Ed is the folksy dad who grows fat in the shadow of his dashing boyfriend. American men grow fat on beer watching Ed. Watching women grow fat dreaming of Johnny. In the radiated blue glow of the vast North American continent the females go to bed with Johnny. Nobody goes to bed with Ed. This doesn't bother Ed: he is fat and rich and can buy himself all the women he wants. He Star Searches. All the little stars come to Poppa's fat and cuddle between his folds: they never really wanted Johnny (except for sex). All the fat men cheer as another starlet drops from the heavens in Santa's lap. Star Search is endless like the universe: there are billions and billions of stars, one for every dollar Ed has. When Ed's Star Search exhausts one galaxy it moves on to another. Fat expands. Cholesterol assimilates the universe. The faraway star where Santa lives is called TV. All good things come to us from TV.

What about Johnny? Is he a proud oak in the shadow of which a fat bubble blossoms? No. Johnny and Ed are one. They cannot be without one another. Johnny provides the simulacrum of psychology to Ed's simulacrum of benevolence. Women need psychology to go to bed, men need fat to stay out of it. Together, Johnny and Ed help the species stay within bounds. Without the hint of child-Johnny no one will go to bed. But without the warmth of cash-fat-Ed there will be no performance. Ed relieves the anxiety Johnny's pseudo-depth suggests. The Johnny in women who goes to bed with the Ed in men is our shallow secret. Johnny is Jack Kennedy going to bed with all the women. Jack is Johnny. Ed is the A-bomb. Oh Ed! Oh Johnny!

When the armored car brings the good news to Ohio as well as the bags of cash, he brings a little piece of the Bomb that insures Peace to the Fatsos. The envious Skinnies who but for the presence of the guard would leap the rails and institute communism are lucky that this is a representative democracy and that Ed was voted Santa. They are lucky because they too are under the protection of Ed the Bomb who lives on TV. There is hope for them yet because they are skinny like Johnny and if it's one thing we've noticed on "Star Search," Marge, is that all the stars or would-be stars are S-K-I-N-N-Y. And that's a fact the rich fatsos will have to put up with after they get over jumping all over their lawn like a herd of elephants. And when they come to they'll want to slim down. They'll want to be steamed and massaged and made young. They'll be using all that money to lose all that fat so patiently grown over years of making their Johnny go to bed with their Ed. And each pound will cost a million; that's six million for each pound for all of 'em. And before you can turn the channel they'll be broke again. But they'll be skinny, no different than their neighbors the Skinnies. By that time, the original Skinnies will have gotten on "Star Search," gained notoriety, lost it and gotten fat. Growing fat allowed them to vote for Santa Ed. Next time the armored truck comes to Ohio it will stop at the former Skinnies' house, and it will be the former Fatsos who will be desperately throwing up their hands and leaping all over the lawn like grasshoppers. That's justice, Ed's justice, which is why we vote for him.

Where does the lost fat go and where does the gained fat come from, since—clearly—it isn't the same fat going from one family to another like a blanket? The gained fat comes from watching Ed on TV while eating the foods that Ed sells. The dog too grows fat eating the food Ed sells. The lost fat goes back to Ed and turns into cash. All the lost fat is Ed's. All the gained fat is also Ed's. There is only one fat owner in the land: Ed, owner of the fat of the land. From Him, who lives on TV engaged in eternal Star Search, comes all Fat and all Fat returns. Santa capitalism wishes you a good night but only if you send in your sweepstakes. If you don't your fat will leave you and then blanket you at the wrong time. The only commodity is timing and Santa's timer is always searching for those who don't watch TV, in order to make them think that day is night and fat is skinny and night is day and skinny is fat and vice versa. This is not punishment but benevolence, not evil but bounty. Tonight when you lie down with Ed's Johnny think of the armored truck sure to come tomorrow.

Cavemen Cry: Film Noir

LIFE WITHOUT TELEVISION IS AN IMPROVEMENT.
Sure, I can't reach for those folksy metaphors in front of a crowd
anymore. And the secret smile in my brain at the Laundromat
when familiar TV words pop out of foreign languages like olives
out of a paella is gone too. Gone too is the certainty that if
captured by the Ladies Auxiliary of Baton Rouge I can talk my
way to freedom with spells out of sitcoms. I lost those things, but
I have gained a fleck of soul. I am less paranoid. I do not suffer the
low-grade anxiety of America anymore. America's true missing
children are the ones watching TV. And I'm saving money because I have not bought a blessed thing advertised on TV since I
quit. Nor have my children, who used to spend *sums*. But beyond
these small liberal victories, I've been having some horrendous
encounters with the world outside the screen.

The only TV-less Americans are scum. You meet them on the
buses. Hitchhiking. Doing the old real American thing. When
America leaves a style behind it doesn't leave it uninhabited. It
leaves it full of horrors. Only desperadoes, freshly freed jailbirds,
yokels going to distant funerals, wetbacks, foreigners and the
entire populations of deinstitutionalized loony bins go Greyhound these days. On the highway there is a new breed of hitch-
hikers, mass murderers and psychos all. A local trio was waltzing
about Louisiana recently raping and killing little girls. Finally one
guy and his girlfriend killed the other guy after sharing a Popeye's
chicken dinner. When they were done eating and stabbing they
cut the guy's hand off and stuck it in the chicken box. They left
the box on a picnic table at a rest area. I've been in that rest area:

some of America's most exotic birds, cranes and storks nest a few feet away.

I've been on a Greyhound too recently. Had the seat in front of the bathroom back of the bus in the smoking (literally) area. In the very last seat was a well battered-mama with tattoos from knees to neck. A handkerchief was holding her withered tits. A pair of terry-cloth hot pants missed her pubic hair by a good tattooed inch, and her bare feet with chipped red toenails rested on the arm of the seat in front of her. Next to her a hairy-chested animal who looked as if he'd *inherited* his tattoos, was snoring. At Baton Rouge in waltzed this mean midget with a face composed of a gang-banged triple-Y gene. His huge arms hung right out of his blue-jean vest and the snakes tattooed on them didn't look any fresher than the ones on the moll and her snoring pound purchase. And where did the scrunched little fuck plant his black ball of hostility? Right. In front of Miss Syphilis and Snarler, and next to yours truly. And without further ado he twisted around, shoving your observer into the corner, and enquired of the withered trollop: "Ya know da Hell's Angels, bitch?"

"Yeah," said the so-addressed, "I been in one of their initiations. You know what that is?"

Even *I* knew what that was, and I prayed that I wouldn't have to hear about it. Someone heard my prayers.

"I been to Ferris Island before they sent me to 'Nam to kill. I killed more people than there are on dis bus. I think they ought to put them niggers, kikes and spics in concentration camps." And so on.

They were getting on famously, at least until the midget staggered to the bathroom with a half-drunk fifth of crummy gin and started retching violently while slapping himself rhythmically and howling racial epithets at his new friend through the open door. All was quiet for a minute, and then a thin cloud of PCP smoke crept under the bathroom door and clouded the five back rows. When he came out he was in a generous mood: he even acknowledged me with a grunt. I grunted back, but there was something suspiciously literate about my grunting because he snarled ferociously and looked about to rip my reading glasses in half. Happily, he took another hit of the PCP joint, and passed the soggy remnant to the social diseases back of us (the illustrated man was awake now). When they were all done with the incinerated horse tranquilizer, the dwarf showed his piece to his new friends. It was a gun about three feet long. The female touched it politely, and said: "It's a *friendly* piece."

The dwarf took offense. He yanked it back, and screamed: "I DON'T NEED NO FUCKIN' FRIENDS!" He pointed the gun at his new friends.

I was experiencing an array of sentiments by now, and so was the whole bus. But unlike the rest of them, I was neither drunk, nor tattooed, nor crazy. Never felt more like a Jew in glasses in my life. (Well, most of my childhood I did but I didn't wear glasses then!)

Luckily, the bus was pulling close to New Orleans, and I was calculating my chances of survival at fifty-fifty. I was also hoping that the sight of the city might inspire the animal with a vague memory of society's repressive arsenal. The little killer interrupted his progression to inevitable mass murder, and ran back to the bathroom for a second retching trip. I leaned over to the T-shirted black guy in front of me and I said: "He needs to be born again!"

The guy turned around to me, a joyful look on his face. I had spoken the right words. "Brother," he said, "I left my Bible in a motel in Hollywood and now they're making a movie from the parts I underlined."

It turned out that he was an itinerant preacher who received mysterious signs pointing out his next destinations, all of which were serviced by Greyhound. He told me that he was originally from Louisiana and he had just gone to visit his parents but couldn't find them because they lived in the swamp in a floating house that kept moving around. No mailman had ever been there twice.

Happily, the dwarf retched long enough for the Dawg to pull into the station, and I shot down the gummy alley like an Ethiopian chicken, the fastest in the world.

One thing about these people, I said to myself when I recovered: they can't be watching too much TV! Or they'd be pacified by now. Lord! They are the last people to live outside the TV screen in America. True, they are the scuzz of the earth, but they are REAL. The last thing I heard the killer dwarf shout before I flew out was: "When the revolution comes I'm gonna put some fuckers away!" And I can just see him, firing away at a TV set. While we look back at him wondrously safe behind the glass.

Of course, you kill everybody on the bus, you won't stay long on the wrong side of the screen. They'll snap you up and set you right before the camera. Still, mass murder isn't what it used to be. Who remembers Son of Sam? The Zodiac Killer? The Santa Cruz Giant? The Black Doodler? Juan Corona? Gacey and Ng? The kidnappers of Chowchilla? Where indeed have they gone among the circuit boards and the silicone isles? It used to be that violent old America had a way in. The crazies could get in through literature (when they found a guy like Kerouac to hitchhike through) or through the news. But now they're doomed to riding the Dawg till doomsday—and many of them do. It costs a hundred bucks to go Greyhound anywhere in this big empty country for a year. That's a year of a warm place to crash and human company. Another hundred buys a year's worth of Popeye's chicken. That's how much a used TV costs and that's one choice that's got to be carefully pondered. You could sit in your floating swamp shack watching your used TV or you can circle America on the Dawg howling the night away. And they'll be making movies from the parts you underlined in that motel Bible long ago, when you could afford it.

The Theatre of Operations in the Drug War Widens: Dispatches from the Front

IN DOWNTOWN LOS ANGELES THE OTHER DAY, I was approached by a street person. "Got a cigarette?" he said, "Or a joint? Or some other stuff?" I didn't, but my friend pulled out her pack of ultrathin Soviet smokes. He took it in his hand, breezed through it briefly, took one out and said: "Don't ever hand your pack to anyone like this. They're bound to find the joint hidden in there." Clearly, the territory around downtown LA is still in the hands of the enemy.

In other parts of the country, however, stunning successes are being reported. In Depew, New York, an eight-year-old boy turned in his mother for allegedly smoking marijuana two days after he listened to President Bush's speech urging children to help people with drug problems. Back when I was growing up behind the Iron Curtain one of my second grade classmates turned his mother in for listening to Radio Free Europe. This was during the Stalinist war on radio. She went to jail and the boy went to an orphans' home. He is now an alcoholic ham-radio operator in a remote village who relays distress signals from lost sailors who want to get back home. The eight year old in Depew is in the custody of his father, while his little brother has been turned over to the child welfare authorities.

In Tres Orejas, New Mexico, a small community is being terrorized by enormous helicopters belonging to the National Guard, which hover over houses scattering children, chicken and livestock. They are looking for the marijuana sure to be found on the rooftops.

The Indianola Academy in Indianola, Mississippi, has just instituted mandatory drug testing for grades one through twelve, and for every teacher and member of the school board. They must submit urine samples on demand. No longer is the student who raises his hand to go to the bathroom certain that he will make it. He may be met halfway there by a man with a tube. It's only the beginning.

Our streets will soon be equipped with little sinks every few feet or so, like the little pooch fountains in Palm Beach. Every twenty minutes, drug patrols will force everyone up against these receptacles. I suggest that these drug patrols be voluntary, so as not to tie up our armed forces which will be busy abroad urine testing foreigners. The Aryan Brotherhood would be an ideal citizens' force for this kind of work, for several reasons, one of them being that they can check to see who's circumcised.

The homefront will be manned by all of us. After the admirable beginning in Depew, children should have no qualms about turning in their parents, spouses should feel free to inform on each other, and, in addition, any one of us should have the right to demand a urine sample from anyone else, in the manner of a citizen's arrest. "Right in here, Daddy! Now!"

Sure, some people will object but, believe me, the psychological problems associated with urination on demand are eminently treatable. I looked up the subject in *The Pill Book: The Illustrated Guide to the Most Prescribed Drugs in the United States,* and there are at least eight medications capable of inducing urination. Of course, that would mean equipping the Aryan Brotherhood with these pills, in addition to flashlight Uzi, litmus paper roll, plungers and blacklist.

My pill book, *The Illustrated Guide to the Most Prescribed Drugs in the United States,* is a wonderful and convincing argument as well for the superiority of legal versus illegal drugs. Did you see the crack-cocaine rocks President Bush had with him on TV? Ugly, wrinkled little things, beaming pure evil! How different

these round, oval, eliptical, square, red, white, pink and multicol-
ored pills neatly stamped by corporate giants. These little pills too
are soldiers in the war against unauthorized drugs. Instead of
helmets, they wear caps. Instead of rifles, they carry medicinal
charges. Many of them are winking at me as I speak. Fire away,
folks!

Sorry, I sometimes get carried away by enthusiasm, and all I
want to do is hang out my proud flag and dream of victory.
Premature dreaming has beset me the way it has the Reagan
administration which also had a war on drugs going for awhile.
That war left us only with the memorable slogan "Just say no!,"
(which was always my philosophy) but little else. Things are
different now. There is a new, more martial spirit, and concrete
results, not just a slogan. Ret. Admiral Crowe, who surprised
everyone by expressing doubts about allowing semiautomatic
weapons to be sold at 7-Elevens, nonetheless put it best when he
said: "Use the army any time anywhere. . . . this is one war that
needs it!"

These signs of success must be very heartening to an administration that once worried about giving a war nobody came to.
They were so worried, in fact, that they staged it at first. The bag
of crack that President Bush held up dramatically during his first
war speech turns out to have been bought by his own people,
who set up the buy as close as they could to the White House.
Well, things like this may have been necessary at first, but now
that children are getting the message, things are OK. When that
eight year old in Depew grows up he can reminisce with the other
veterans about the early sacrifices.

When I was but a mere child myself, I spent long days day-
dreaming about winning over bad guys. I used to float away on
summer afternoons off our hot stone porch in the Carpathians,
and feel my spirit rise right over the mountains holding the flame
of righteousness in its beaming hand. My body, left behind like
a lizard skin, was flat and still like the skin of our lake. By the lake
shore, old women beat the seeds out of hemp and smoked long
stogies made from the leaves. Now and then their singing would

rise over the water. At the Black Sea coast, where I spent my summers, old Turkish men sat at outdoor cafés in the evening with their glowing hookahs lighting up their faces. They told funny jokes about hashish smokers and drinkers, two opposing species. The drinkers always got the worst of it. They lost their wives and their treasures to the *hashisheens*.

During my grim adolescence in the grainy police state of Romania, I used to shut my eyes very tightly and hit both my temples with my fists in order to transcend the place. I sometimes saw brightly colored stars through the headache, and imagined a world of color somewhere.

That world came finally one day in Rome, Italy, a week after I had flown the commie coop in 1965, in the form of a rain shower of gold that gilded all the monuments near the Piazza Navona, and shocked my whole being with the revelation that the world is a living, shimmering fabric that every living creature is part of. The world, I realized, was made of vibrant living substance, not tiny submachine guns. (Although I did later run into some Czech substance that held to the image of a universe composed entirely of tiny sickles and hammers.)

I was an enemy, I guess.

But I wasn't the only one. The story of evolution is not gradual, as everyone knows by now. There are sudden leaps caused by radical changes of consciousness. These leaps are induced by drugs. Everything in nature likes to induce consciousness change. (May indeed be under an imperative to do so). Birds go crazy eating fermented berries, horses like their apples just after they've left the cider stage, Greek gods sit around Olympus with smoke coming out of their nostrils, and Christianity is, of course, a mushroom cult.

There are a lot of enemies out there.

Victory in the war against drugs is an elusive goal, especially if one has to also fight all the animals. But then, again, the current campaign has wisely set itself more modest initial goals. At the beginning this war will be only against young black men who tend to damage property under the influence of cocaine. If they were reading German instead, they would all be Sigmund Freuds, not vandals. But since there is no money for German lessons and trips to Vienna, we'll put them in jail instead. (Of course, there are alternatives to jail, one of which was suggested to me by a bartender: "Throw a cement wall around the ghetto! Put guard towers every twenty feet!")

Wars can get out of hand though, so the objectives may soon widen. I mean, first the metaphor gets out of hand, then the killing gets loud. And when you set up a large police machinery with a need for action you'll soon outgrow the originally limited objectives. Once the structure is in place it demands food. More files! More raids! More enemy! There is never enough enemy to go around when you have a shiny new structure that feeds on blood. After running out of drug dealers, users and sympathizers, it will start demanding radicals, liberals, Democrats and people with reading glasses. I am willing to bet anything that, at this very moment, one of the more immediate activities of the war is the resurrection of old 1960s files in the deep memory of the NSA, FBI, CIA, army and navy counterintelligence and the hundreds of secret regional outfits who have been gathering painful dust during peacetime. Imagine the glee of reactivated agents blowing dust off the yellowed folders like mini-Poseidons starting up gales. In there are the true hidden cores of now respectable citizens! We'll get them all: this is war! You didn't think that the entire nation has been mobilizing for the purpose of keeping a few black teenagers from crossing the freeway? Or keeping a few Colombian farmers from exceeding the import quota?

After that, we'll get the animals. In spite of our best efforts to eradicate them, the animals are still out there getting high.

No Tacos for Saddam!: Memories of the Gulf War

IT'S OVER NOW, THE WORLD'S FIRST POSTMODERN war, and verily, the righteous are upon us like fleas on a corpse or buzzards on a road kill. The boom of the cannons and the whistling of the jets is still ringing in ears as the patriots and the victors rejoice.

The Presbyterian church on the corner has for its sermon-subject this Sunday: THE MAN WHO ROWS THE BOAT DOESN'T GENERALLY ROCK IT. Take that all you boat rockers, critics of our mighty nation and our glorious prezident! The righteous and the uncritical, the faithful and the unquestioning are the victors! It's the hour of triumph for the obedient grudge who pulls on those oars with all his simpleminded might. He cares not who owns the boat, who launched him on the perilous water or what cargo he's carrying—his job is to row, row, row that boat of state.

Notice however the word "generally." The man who rows the boat does not "generally" rock it. Now and then it does happen—we must sadly admit it—that one of the meek, tired of rowing, stands up and begins to rock. But rarely—these days. Everyone's cockier these days. Americans stand taller today, says the TV commentator, and verily, it is true. Taller than ever Americans drive their jeeps on the streets as if every pedestrian was an Iraqi. Blond guys in line at the Taco Bell shove rudely in front of dark guys with mustaches. No tacos for Saddam!

AMERICA THE GREAT says every bumper sticker, T-shirt and college boy. And that's all you'll ever need to know, never mind the fact that some of these guys move their lips to read their own T-shirts. Every patriot's earned the right to be more obnoxious now. Life is at its simplest now with the boat all decked in yellow ribbons being rowed into the harbor of Pax Americana—or the Exxon loading dock. Yes, and verily, things are hunky-dory now before the boat rockers begin once again noting things like the blood-covered oars and the shackles on the rowers' wrists, and the cost of the trip . . . later for that, stand proud now!

Yes, the first postmodern war is over and the ratings were good, even though David Lynch had his friends write to the networks because they kept interrupting "Twin Peaks."

The postmodern war was very postmodern, a perfect package neatly packaged, but there was disappointment naturally that it didn't go a few more rounds. In that respect the war was like the World Series last year, over in four games, leaving the networks with all that time on their hands.

The postmodern war, just like sci-fi writers predicted, resembled the virtual reality games played in game rooms all over America by boys with lasers. The lopsided score, 40 to 100 thousand, further underlined the eerie postmodernity of this war unlike the last modern war, WWII, when the scores were pretty even until we introduced the postmodern weapon at Hiroshima and Nagasaki.

In the postmodern war they died and we didn't see them.

In the postmodern war they died and nobody saw them on TV.

In the postmodern war they died and never saw their death coming.

In the postmodern war the "they" who died were called "the attrited" and the "corollary targets."

The postmodern war was such a neat package that when it came to our door, neatly tied with a yellow ribbon, we never thought twice before signing the receipt. Those who didn't sign were soundly trounced with wet bunting and driven to hide when the victorious postmodern warriors came home on TV to fireworks and parades. The success of the spectacle was the safety of the spectacle and the spectacle continues to be spectacular so that even though the war itself didn't produce enough programming, the postwar celebrations should fill the gaps just fine.

In the postmodern world to come all future shows will be planned for way ahead of time to avoid any sudden onset of dead air. Dead air is premodern air, filled with the unpredictable shouts of anguished humanity. Postmodern air is the air in the bubble inside the airtight chamber of virtual reality. In the end, the word "reality" will have to go because it reminds us of something we'd rather not remember. "Virtuality" 'll have to do.

Did this war have any heroes? Can someone with a blinking screen and a bomb be called a hero if he hits the video target? Why, he played hundreds of such games in the lunchroom or after school and nobody called him a hero *then*. Of course, then there was no BD (bomb damage) and BDA.

But there were heroes, though no official ones.

Hail, Fabrice Moussus, ABC News cameraman who defied orders to crawl into the bunker, and shot pictures of the glittering night sky of Baghdad under bombs! After this feat, Fabrice and three others drove twenty-four straight hours through allied bombardments to Jordan, where they delivered their spectacular film canisters! Fabrice's feat was almost without precedent in the near-total darkness of censorship that descended over our media in the Persian Gulf.

I know Fabrice from Romania. This past July he shot a segment for "Nightline" about my visit there. The segment was never aired because Iraq invaded Kuwait. Fabrice went immediately to Baghdad with Ted Koppel.

I liked Fabrice. A suave, worldly, charming Frenchman famous for his sangfroid and his exploits—he was the only cameraman to have filmed the Anwar Sadat assassination—he was also a first-class teacher. Seated at one of Bucharest's most elegant restaurants, he commented that we could be in Paris. He took great care in choosing the wine, asking the maître d' pertinent and sophisticated questions in one of the several languages he knew. When I remarked to him that I was beginning to lose mental contact with the people I knew back home, he reassured me gently. "It's all right," he said, "it's a good thing to be exactly where you are." I felt at that moment that he was indeed at home, enjoying himself enormously, filled with the mystery and the strangeness of the place, at home in the unfamiliar.

I watched him later converse with an old German gentleman in a cafe in Transylvania, charm a seventeen-year-old Romanian beauty in witty French, and instruct his crew in flawless English. His American-born sound man Dennis followed behind Fabrice's camera like a dancer. The two of them were a perfectly synchronized and graceful duo. When he set up his shots Fabrice had a lightning-fast way of appraising the scene and quickly finding the most dramatic stage. He posed me in front of a row of machine-gun toting soldiers of the interior ministry guarding the Parliament building in Bucharest, and out of all those soldiers he found the meanest-looking one. He sent our producer, Reed, to offer the man a cigarette. The soldier refused, but the transaction took just long enough for Fabrice to get his shot. By the time the soldier made a threatening gesture we were already out of there.

During those first dark days of the war when the media seemed to have achieved negative apotheosis—a total sense of crisis with a near-total lack of news—Fabrice Moussus's refreshing insouciance was heartening. He reminded us of a time when newsmen were heroes.

Every night, as I watched my tax dollars go up in smoke, I couldn't shake the suspicion that smoke was all I was getting. There were no spontaneous pictures from the front, no footage unstamped by the military.

What went on here? Never was so much coverage spent on so much nothing, unless you consider the bulldog faces of ex-generals and so-called "experts" something. There they went like ex-football players dragged out of retirement to comment on the latest sports event produced by the Pentagon, an event, alas, invisible to the naked eye.

Censorship, and varieties thereof, is what we got for the 350 million to 2 billion dollars blown to smithereens every day in the desert. For that money, we got U.S. military censorship, Israeli censorship, Iraqi censorship, Saudi censorship and the media's own self-censorship. You would think that all this censorship would have left time for something else, but no, our time and attention were also being ripped off.

No one noticed, for instance, the bit about Manuel Noriega getting bags of cash from the CIA and the U.S. Army, a rather timely item considering that the last war we wasted billions on what was waged for the purpose of capturing Noriega. . . .

And what of the purpose of *this* war? Don't even ask! We were too busy watching simulations of video games and enriching our vocabularies with the lovely names of mass-destruction weapons like SCUD and TOMAHAWKS. . . . any kid can now tell you what those deadly toys can do, but nobody can tell you what they've actually done. . . . because that's still secret.

I don't know what you call it when somebody takes your money and doesn't tell you what they've done with it. . . . *highway robbery* is one thing that comes to mind.

And while we played our all-consuming video game for real cash, the bad guys were all having a great time just out of hearing range. . . . Soviet troops killed unarmed Lithuanian and Latvian demonstrators. . . . Syrians consolidated their stranglehold on Lebanon. . . . China got back trade agreements without a murmur about democracy. . . . who remembered democracy anyway when we were putting on a mighty weapons display to restore a medieval monarchy? They even talked about canceling the Super Bowl and Mardi Gras, but that depended, of course, on the ratings.

Happily, they didn't cancel Mardi Gras.

Mardi Gras was on although it was decided to add yellow to the traditional Mardi Gras green and purple on the banners.

Yellow ribbons were already tied to every tree on St. Charles Avenue, making the old oaks look like overbred poodles. I'd always thought yellow stood for cowardice as in "you're yellow," but in this case it was patriotism driving the ribbon tiers, although I suspected patriotism was only a small part of it here in the deep South where decorating anything from a cake to a head is a blind passion. Some young women here wear bows the size of helicopter blades in their hair. Whenever more than three of these "bow heads" sit together they look like a chopper fleet ready for takeoff.

Anyway, Mardi Gras was safe, and the first parade unrolled through the French Quarter with customary panache. It was the Parade of the Vieux Carre, organized by the *krewe* of CRUDE or the Council to Revive Urban Decadence and Entertainment, an umbrella group composed of the *krewes* of Mystic Inane, Space Age Love, Underwear, the Gemini Visionary Society, the Pardon my French Social and Pleasure Club, and others I don't recall. The themes this year were varied but the spirit of the times could be gleaned when LOST—the Louisiana Organization of Stool Teachers—paraded a huge butt-naked Saddam Hussein with a Patriot missile heading for his exposed hinterland. The inflated Saddam was followed by the Genitalia of the Rich and Famous who paraded with foam-rubber head dresses and political masks. Ronald Reagan went by with a bobbing missile penis. Some marchers threw peas at the crowd and sang John Lennon's "Give Peas a Chance." A beer-soaked couple from the provinces huddled close together watching the irreverent passage, and the wife said: "My God, can you imagine what *Mardi Gras*'s gonna look like? It's still days early . . ."

She had a point. While the world was going insane, Mardi Gras was the sanest thing going.

And now that we've attrited all the enemy, we're going to have the New World Order.

In the New World Order there will be no more disorder, that much we know. All those people who litter, laze, sprawl and don't do a lick of work in all those countries that don't function too efficiently because everybody takes siestas all the time, all those slow-on-the-uptake countries with all their low-producing un-work-ethical people, will become efficient, clean and productive when the New World Order comes. No more piddling around.

Before the New World Order here in the United States we had the New Age, which was OK, but there wasn't enough order in it. That's over now.

Throughout history there were many attempts at New Order. There was Hitler's New Order, there was Nixon's Law and Order, there was *Novus Ordo Seclorum*—that we still have, it's on the dollar bill—and the Communist boy scouts' Order and Discipline.

The New World Order will bring to millennial fruition the eternal calls of school teachers for "order in the classroom," and the heart-wrenching cries of the world's silent majorities for "peace, quiet and order."

The New World Order will be enforced, maintained and kept in the forefront of all our activities by the world's greatest, best and most expensive technocop, the U.S. military. President Bush in a speech referring to the New World Order called the twentieth century the twentieth "central" by mistake. But maybe it wasn't a mistake, but a reference to the way the New World Order will divide the world into a number of "centrals." In these centrals there will be order. Everyone else gets sent to extraterrestrial penal colonies.

The New World Order is related to "orderly behavior," "your order, Sir," "ordering before you go out," "we have our orders," and "order in the courtroom." The New World Order will mean very special things to every field of endeavor, area of life and geographical region.

In my case, for instance, it will mean "rhyme and reason," and "clean living" in "crime-free New Orleans." As you can see, I've already started.

And I will end my war memories on a personal note. Not many people know this and perhaps not many people *should* know this, but baseball was invented in Transylvania by Romanian sheepherders. It was called *oina*, it was played with a stick and a ball, and it was introduced to this country by Romanian immigrants to New York. There is an Oina Federation in Romania dedicated to maintaining and propagating the sport.

I had forgotten this earth-shattering fact until I got a call from a man named Sorin Băleanu, a former wrestling champion from Romania who wanted to tell me about yet another sport invented by Romanians: foot tennis. Băleanu started a foot tennis foundation here in the United States and he plans to make foot tennis the sport of the nineties. I remember playing foot tennis with these really bad guys who smoked cigarettes in a vacant lot behind the school. It was a great sport to be associated with because only the toughest guys played it.

Anyway, I only mention this because sports are going to be bigger than ever now after the war. Not many people realize this, but two of the forces that confronted each other during this war were Sport and Art. Sport won—by the lopsided score of 40 to 100 thousand—and Art lost.

I'd already had a hint of this shortly before the war when my friend Barry Gifford, who's a novelist, called to tell me that he turned down an invitation to the Stockholm Film Festival to come my way for the LSU-Ole Miss game.

But while it is true that sports will be bigger than ever, they won't be the same kind of prewar sports. The postwar sports will be more sophisticated, more technical and more simpleminded at the same time.

There will also be more at stake so all kinds of ominous elements will be introduced, things like laser helmets and shoes with *real* wings, and the complete disappearance of the losers to the strains of the latest Judas Priest CD. In that sense, anything new out of Transylvania should be a big success.

In a way, Sport will be more like Art in the near future in the way that Judas Priest is like Goethe's Young Werther, same result, different styles.

See you in the vacant lot.

Torture and the Dream
of the Bourgeois

THEY HAD A SPECIAL ON TORTURE AT THE LOCAL Woolworth's and I had two. No, what I mean is I was going to write this piece on torture because I had an interesting dream about it, but every time I get started I get this pain. There *is* a part of the dream I don't remember: that's the part where one of the tech guys probably said: *If you whisper a word of this to anyone* . . . Anyway, there I was, with a bunch of friends, and our kids, waiting in line to be tortured. It was no big deal. In fact, a kind of festive atmosphere prevailed. It was understood by all present that torture was just this thing we all had to undergo, like a vaccine or a measles shot. They first took the kids. They had a long, somewhat distorted sort of room, the kind you see at science exhibits with funny floors and windows. It was full of toys. The kids dug it first when it started shaking, but after a while it shook harder and harder and they were still trying to believe for all they were worth that this was fun, but it wasn't.

After about an hour, it stopped. Then it was my turn. There was a doctor and a nurse, and they had the most pleasant manner. They had tourniquets and wheels and things, and lots of stainless steel sinks. The guy who came out as I was going in was pretty shaken. "When they turn the numbers on that crank," he said, "You'll tell them everything." I felt like telling them everything anyway, before they even started. I had an idea of what this crank with numbers looked like: like a plumber's pliers with a spiked wheel on it. And I didn't want it. But by and by, the pleasant couple had me at ease and all tied up. I woke up.

I'm not new to suffering. Just the other day I was having coffee with my most cheerful friend, Jannie, and I said: "I'm being tortured." "Pshaw!," she said, "I have a Ph.D. in suffering!" Who would have guessed? Hiding under that cheerful exterior was an expert in suffering. Makes you leary of bright A.M.s.

But my dream torture was something else. I gained a clue from Ruth Montgomery, whose book *The Walk-Ins* I keep at my bedside along with Sandie Castle's *The Catholics Are Coming*. Ruth says that Walk-Ins, who are dead people coming to inhabit the living in order to prepare our orderly evacuation from our bodies during the upcoming giving up of ghost en masse, are arriving at the rate of 10,000 a day in the New York–Washington, D.C. area. She claims that the Walk-Ins only take over a living person if the living person is sick of living. But I have a feeling that because of emergency preparations a lot of the living are being taken over against their will. It is also possible that many of these discorporated beings are former Nazis, and they are taking over the way they know best. Can you see the ghost of Dr. Mengele asking the okay of a Romanian Jew? Torture may well be a very strong addiction, not curable by death.

The return of torture, as documented by human rights groups, is a certainty among the living. After a short period of being discredited, it has made a strong comeback. There was Argentina, a real laboratory of torture before the fall of the army, and there is El Salvador, Iraq, and probably every place you can think of, in varying degrees. Why now? Why torture? What can be gained by torture that can't be ferreted out electronically or voluntarily? The answer: nothing. Torture isn't being used to any ends: it is an art. Torture for torture's sake. In many cases, the information isn't worth the buckets of spurting blood or the smell of fried hair. The victims are killed anyway, whether they talk or not.

The occasional revelations of sadistic cults dedicated to nothing more than the humiliation of the body suggest that a kind of numbness has set in us. One way to *feel* something is torture. The other is to fall in love: after a period of intoxication, that too becomes torture. But there are differences of degree, of course.

Semiofficial torture is to lovers' torture what the jet plane is to the horse cart. And then there is the being-tortured-at-a-boring-poetry-reading-kind-of-torture, which is to the jet and to the horse cart what gasoline is to the whip.

There is a class aspect to my dream: I was being tortured for being in the middle class. (Or at least the torturer-initiators thought so). There is an initiation rite when a bohemian enters the middle class: he or she is tortured in dreams. The only cure is to give it up. In other words, buy nothing. Breathe the air.

I am not interested in masochism. It has never had the slightest appeal to me. I think masochists are slimy little scumbags who have to control everything, including the amount of pain that's being inflicted on their pitiful rolls of flesh. Masochism is only vaguely related to torture. No masochist will yield his power to something as absolute as torture. Sadists, on the other hand, are even more disgusting: they think of themselves as saviors. They make their victims *feel*. How therapeutic. Which is why the white coats and the stainless steel sinks. But whatever their mettle and pedigree, both the purveyors and the dishers of pain are on the increase.

When they show up in dreams, it's serious. It could be the beginning of the Next World War, after the Cold War. The new enemies are Ghost Nazis.

III *The Suicide of Communism*

Workers of the World, Disperse!
ANARCHIST SLOGAN

Havel to the Castle!
PRAGUE, 1989

Romania Today: A Bad Novel

IF YOU ASK AN AMERICAN TODAY WHAT HE OR SHE knows about Romania, you are likely to hear that it is a country full of abandoned children ruled until recently by Dracula and now ruled by miners, and also a country which gave the world a great playwright, Eugène Ionesco, and a great gymnast, Nadia Comaneci.

This is not an entirely inaccurate description, even at the metaphorical level: Romania *is* a country of abandoned children, literal children and grown-up children, abandoned by its own leadership, by the West and, psychologically, by its own citizens. It is a country sucked dry by Dracula-Ceauşescu. And whenever its citizens try to take responsibility for their destiny there come, as if from the depths of a weird fairy-tale, coal-streaked miners with nightsticks. Our great playwright, Ionesco, founded the Theatre of the Absurd because the Absurd is still the chief functioning mechanism there. But perhaps Romania resembles nothing more than our Olympian wonder, Nadia Comaneci. Like Nadia, Romania was once known for its charm, its grace and its ability to perform miracles on the balancing beam of history. This may be a myth but it was a potent and useful one until recently. Like Nadia, Romania lost its reputation for flexibility and magic in a single bound. When Nadia defected to the U.S. and stuck her tongue out in defiance at the press she lost instantly millions of dollars in possible commercial endorsements. When Romania showed the world its neo-communist post-December government and its miners, it likewise lost its credibility.

Romania today is a bad detective novel, a *roman policier* written by too many writers, plotted by too many atrocious scribblers, edited by hacks, published on bad paper by people without respect for timing, characters or readers—an exercise in embarrassment.

I am not using this metaphor lightly.

Questions about the events of December 1989, June 1990 and October 1991 revolve continually about the idea of "script." How much of what we saw on television in December of 1989 was scripted, how much of it was spontaneous? How many Securitate men with scripts in hand led around the miners in 1990 and 1991?

These kind of literary questions eventually create their own weather, they magnetize all circumstances toward their logic. I was a presenter at the Emmy Awards for Broadcast Journalism in New York in September 1991. I presented an Emmy Award to the producers of "Nobody's Children," a television documentary about the tragic situation of Romanian orphans. This was powerful television, but I kept thinking even as I was performing the ceremony that it's a shame and a pity that Romania is now known in the U.S. almost exclusively for its orphans. "I must be the first Romanian," I said, "to present an Emmy Award for television, but that's only fitting since we gave you the world's first tele-revolution." Well, some three presenters later, a man climbed on stage to present another Emmy, and he said: "I must be the second Romanian to give out an Emmy, and I *produced* the world's first tele-revolution." That was our ambassador to the United Nations, Mr. Aurel Dragoş-Munteanu, a man I first met in 1964 when he was editor of the literary journal *Luceafărul*, and I was a young poet reading my poems in the Luceafărul Workshop. I saw him again in 1989 when he became spokesman for the government, during a press conference at the Intercontinental Hotel in Bucharest. At that time he drew the attention of foreign journalists to a question asked by a Romanian journalist. The question was: "Why is Romania selling its children?" In 1964, Mr. Munteanu was a writer of fiction. "Eventually," he told me later that evening of the Emmys in New York, "I am going to write novels about these events; the reality is too unbelievable."

Now, I wasn't sure then and I'm not sure now what fiction

and reality he had in mind. The reality brought about by the initial fiction he helped create on TV? A reality that he could only discuss by re-fictionalizing it?

Prior to the Age of Orphans-Miners, among readers in the West, Romania was also known for the brilliance of its writers, particularly its poets. There was an undisputed consensus that imagination flourished in the Carpathians and that it gave birth to a complex poetry. In other words, we were not known for the ingenuity of our sciences, our social or political wisdom, the probity of our international relations or the integrity of our leaders—we were known and admired mostly for the brilliance of our culture. The world, to be sure, did not read very much of our brilliant literature, not as much as it read Czech, Polish or Soviet writers, but the perception was nonetheless there, based on a number of exiled poets, all of whom were Romanian Jews: Tristan Tzara, Paul Celan, Ilarie Voronca, Benjamin Fondane, Gherasim Luca, and Eugène Ionesco, who is half-Jewish. In addition they knew us also by the writings of Mircea Eliade and Emil Cioran, who may not formally be Jews but philosophically and temperamentally, in their bitterness and humor, could be considered as such since their preoccupations with exile and estrangement brought them willy-nilly into the sphere of Jewish concerns.

I make this point because among the tremendous damages that Romania's image has sustained since December 1989, one of the greatest is the rise of a crude and vicious anti-Semitism that is horrifying the civilized world. This anti-Semitism is partly fostered by the rise of nationalist groups such as "Vatra Romaneasca" and "Romania Mare," which are supported by Ceauşescu's old fascist-Communist secret police. But only partly. This virulent racism may also be a manifestation of the character of many people raised under Ceauşescu's national-socialist regime. Wouldn't it be horrific if the New Socialist Man, that ideal creature dreamt of in the Communist fictions, actually existed in Romania? This is an unexplored area of the psyche of contemporary Romania, which may not be unique to us. The same phenomenon, in various degrees, has occurred in all of Eastern Europe and the Soviet

Union. The chief psychological traits of this animal would be: thuggery (for which the Romanian word *smecherie* may be accurate), cynicism, servility, stupidity, lack of culture, lack of moral values, an inability to function without "directives," and a great inarticulate anger. The embodiments of these traits may be average citizens, not something as exceptional as the so-called "miners," who are, it appears, proto-human or maybe post-human, something between, let's say, an ape and a communist. I am saying this also because I was raised in Communist Romania—nineteen years of my life—and I am able to identify quite precisely these characteristics in various unthinking aspects of my thinking. It took me years in the West to speak of political matters in a normal tone of voice. When I didn't lower it, I shouted too loud. How then can people who have used various subsonic tones of voice to communicate important things suddenly begin a reasonable political discourse? It's a question being debated both in Romania and abroad, a question the answers to which are forthcoming from writers who are, it seems to me, the only people capable of articulating them.

But not any writers, of course. "Every Romanian is a poet," goes an old saw, and given the extraordinary proliferation of scripts, scenarios, fabulations and fantasies it would certainly appear that way. Most of the fabulists responsible for inventing recent Romanian history are, however, very bad poets. The poets of Securitate and of the National Salvation Front, together with their "legitimate" scribblers, people like Eugen Barbu and C. V. Tudor are completely without merit. Theirs is the poetry of labor camps, torture and conspiracy, the nonpoetic poetry of the police mind.

We look with envy and regret at those countries, Czechoslovakia and Hungary, in particular, where the good writers did in fact manage to play great roles. Why not Romania? I ask myself. Our good writers are as good as theirs. But maybe the Czechs and the Poles and the Hungarians don't have as *many* poets. Maybe their policemen and apparatchiks did not think of themselves as poets. Maybe not everyone should be a poet.

Given the hallucinatory nature of the new reality of Romania in 1991, together with a certain national propensity for paradox and poetry, how can one best describe recent history? What *did* happen in December 1989 when there was a "hole in the flag," and a so-called "revolution"?

I wrote a book about it, and all I can tell you is that I'm glad I wrote the book when I did—in 1990—because if I knew then what I know now I couldn't have written it. In the simplicity of my innocence I followed two criteria: the evidence of my senses, and published reports. Neither, as I see it now, were very reliable guides. The evidence of my senses was based on two trips I took to Romania: one at the end of December 1989 and one in June 1990, shortly after the *mineriada*, which is the wonderful Romanian word for describing the epic disaster of the miners' attack on Bucharest on June 13–15, 1990.

In December, I was overwhelmed, as the entire world was, by the riveting spectacle of a mass uprising against the dictatorship of Ceauşescu, an uprising that was crystallized by certain powerful images, chief among which was the hole in the flag, which became the title of my book. This hole, made in the Romanian tricolor by cutting out the socialist emblem put there by the Communists symbolized many things: a break with the past, an opening to the world, an ingress and an egress into what had been an airless, oppressive world. Seeing Romanian flags with the hole cut out fluttering from the tops of tanks and buildings was an intoxicating sight.

I wrote in my book that it was through this hole that I was returning to my birth-country after twenty-five years in exile. The euphoric chaos of those days was unforgettable. In that hole, that brief vacuum between Ceauşescu and Iliescu, a great celebration went on. Voices stilled for decades were suddenly heard in the vacated space, the voices of millions of people silenced by the secret police. Everyone felt the need to confess, profess, shout, narrate and expound. Strangers on the street told each other their deepest secrets. The magnetic attraction of the world's cameras and microphones—unlike the cameras and microphones of Securitate—drew out the great reservoirs of speech that had been locked up for years. One man took hold of my microphone and recited into it all the names of American presidents that he knew—until my exasperated producer had to stop him because we had other things to do. But he wouldn't let go: "Taft, Coolidge, Hoover . . ."

Vast masses of people mobbed the streets in front of the Romanian TV station, demanding to speak their stories. A young woman holding high a tape cassette said that she had on there a song for her country, a song that did not yet have words or music, but that she was sure that once inside the TV station, there would be people who could easily fix that. She was right. Inside the TV station there *were* people who could provide her song with words and music but these were not the words or the music that either her or millions of Romanians wanted to hear. The words that the profiteers of the great spontaneous uprising were going to affix to her song were words like,"Stop Thinking, Start Working!," "Long live Iliescu and the National Salvation Front!," and the music, well, the music was that of nightsticks breaking over the heads of young people, students and workers, who wanted to keep the hopes of December alive.

Together with the hole in the flag, there was an array of other images. The bodies of Nicolae and Elena Ceauşescu, lying shot dead on the dirty cement of a small schoolhouse where their so-called "trial" took place. Incidentally, the words "so-called" will have to be attached to great many totemic labels of Romania's recent events. There is the "so-called revolution," the "so-called miners," the "so-called democratization," the "so-called privatization," and even my "so-called high school reunion" in June 1990. Other images: hundreds of thousands of people massed in the streets of Timisoara chanting "EUROPE IS WITH US," (*EUROPA E CU NOI!*), and, simultaneously, "GOD EXISTS!" (*DUMNEZEU EXISTA*); army tanks with fresh-faced young soldiers on top of them fraternizing with the ecstatic mobs; the bodies of young heroes murdered in Timisoara and Bucharest; the young mother with her baby at her breast lying on a cobblestone Timisoara street, both of them killed by a single bullet.

In the lengthy analysis undertaken after December by more

sober people, many of these images appeared as less than spontaneous, while others were dismissed altogether. The chanting
crowds were doubtlessly animated by the sincere desire to be done
with the Ceauşescus, but not only with the Ceauşescus, but also
with the System. They wanted an end to the red fascist dictatorship that had been holding them under its boot for four and a
half decades. The fresh-faced young soldiers on tanks were another matter. The army, which had skillfully fostered the myth of
"The Army is With Us," (*"Armata E Cu Noi"*) may in fact had
been guilty of most of the murders of unarmed demonstrators
on the streets. The secret police (Securitate) was undoubtedly
responsible for killing as well and, in fact, most of the dead were
probably the result of shoot-outs between rival Securitate gangs,
and army and Securitate. In Sibiu, a number of traffic cops were
labelled "terrorists" by the army and shot in their building even
though they had surrendered. Those arrested had to be released.

The news media, of which I was a part (I was reporting on
Romania for both National Public Radio and ABC News) made
itself an unthinking carrier of these and other images originating
in Romania until the world believed that a great civil war was
raging in that country. This perception caused French president
Mitterrand to call for the formation of an international brigade
like in the Spanish Civil War, to aid the Romanian freedom
fighters. This call was echoed by our secretary of state James
Baker, who said that we were not adverse to Soviet intervention
on the right side. Surreal though these perceptions may be, they
testify to the initial success of those who plotted the so-called
"revolution" in Romania. When some facts later came to light,
such as the exaggerated numbers of victims, the faked video,
the staged "spontaneity" of the formation of the National Salvation Front, and of the provisional government, many newsmen
including myself were embarrassed. The governments, however,
were not. There was no apology from Mr. Baker, for instance,
who should have known that what Romanians hated more than
Ceauşescu were Soviet troops.

During my late December, early January stay in Romania the

airwaves were suffused with this imagery. The evidence of my senses, as I've said before, was also that great, irreversible, fabulous changes had occurred and that Romania could look hopefully to the future. Among Romanian writers, the euphoria was tempered with any numbers of cautionary notes. An old friend, a novelist, told me that "too many people are coming out of anonymity too soon." At the Writers' Union where I had coffee with Mircea Dinescu, the new union president, and Ana Blandiana, I heard how the old Ceauşescu faces were already reappearing in public life. As to how best to proceed, opinions differed. In the absence of facts, other imaginative functions were at work.

One key to understanding what has taken place in Romania, and what has happened to Romania's international reputation, is literature. The tele-revolution was scripted by people who knew how to use tape (both audio and video), how to edit, how to provide a narrative continuity. Listening to citizens in their homes and cars, filming them walking through the parks, editing the tape for review is an evolved skill that with the aid of a little imagination can fool the whole world. And it did. When and if Securitate, and their clones throughout Eastern Europe and the former Soviet Union, become truly unemployed, they will all go to writing programs in schools to get degrees in fiction. Unfortunately for them, fortunately for us, the fiction or fictions that the anonymous writers of Romania's Ceauşist-fascist secret police have created are confusing, murky, filthy and unpalatable to the civilized world. Meanwhile, the "real" writers, those who maintained "the authentic values" of literature throughout the years of the dictatorship, are being purposefully excluded from the future of the country by a government of police-puppets. Romanian writers are working harder now than at any time during the dictatorship. At a time when their counterparts in the former Eastern bloc are enjoying the very real job of shaping their countries' futures, our creative minds are mired in the foul aftermath of police fictions, afloat in a hopeless world of fractured facts, suffocated by the demands of a journalism that is, alas, only too necessary.

In conclusion, until the factual truth is somehow brought out and clarified, until the writers of the numerous plots that have destroyed our country's image abroad are brought to justice, until the damage to the psyche of the average person is somehow assessed, until two generations of fat opportunistic managers are swept out of farms and factories, until Romanians stop hating Jews, Gypsies and Hungarians . . . until, until, until then . . . we will stay still within our vortex of fairy tales. . . . stuck in an "once upon a time," more punishing than "all this happened because I was there." Romania ought to be given a chance to *begin*.

This speech was delivered on October 21, 1991. It was the inaugural lecture for the Ratiu Chair in Romanian Studies at Georgetown University in Washington, D.C. In the audience were some very interesting people. The Romanian ambassador could not attend, but sent his regrets through the cultural attaché, Mr. Andrei Busuioceanu who, to his credit, stayed until the very end and even shook my hand. It is a pity that the ambassador did not come himself because he could have met Mr. John Davis, the new U.S. ambassador to Romania who did attend, and Mrs. Ballabas, the information officer at the Hungarian embassy. I was gratified to see in the audience Mr. Vladimir Tismaneanu, who is one of the most brilliant Romanian scholars in English. Also there were Mr. Nestor Ratesh from Radio Free Europe, and the heads of several foundations concerned with Romania. Sitting rather uncomfortably at the back I noticed the portly figure of Father Calciu, who did not applaud and left immediately afterwards. The question and answer period that followed the talk was very interesting as well. Two questions stick in my mind: "Should Romania receive the most favored nation clause from the U.S.?" (Ambassador Davis) I said that I mostly thought "no" because of the scoundrels in power, and that sometimes I thought "yes" if it would improve the lives of average Romanians. That "yes", however, should be qualified by some very strict guarantees. The other question was, "Is it true that Hungarians want Transylvania?" I replied that none of the Hungarians I spoke to ever hinted at any territorial ambitions toward Romania, and that, in fact, they were emphatic about this point. I said that I did not doubt that there were right-wing extremists in Hungary who, like their counterparts in Romania, fostered hate and division. Happily, these extremists are a marginal movement in Hungary. Not so the Romanian extremists who are mainstream.

Writing Without the Enemy: The First Postrevolutionary Issue of România Literară

HOLDING IN MY HANDS THE DECEMBER 28, 1989 issue of *România Literară*, issue number fifty-two, year twenty-two, is a sharp double-barreled pleasure. Here it is, the same indifferent quality paper, small letters and nearly identical format as the journal of my youth which I used to purchase at the corner newsstand from a nasty dwarf who secretly liked me. I used to scan *RL*'s small type twenty-five years ago in search first of my name (in the "Editorial Mail," a column that answered publicly all and sundry), then for the names of my friends. If we were in there, fine. If not, we blamed it on censorship. The almost inexpressible pleasure of fifty-two, year twenty-two, is the fact that it's the first uncensored issue.

Unlike other Romanian publications following the December 1989 revolution, *RL* changed neither its name nor its number. After the revolution there was an orgy of name changing, a symbolic festival that took in everything from the name of the country—which became Romania from the Socialist Republic of—to newspapers and institutes. All the newly renamed journals began blithely with volume one, issue number one—sometimes qualified by the words "new series"—as if they had sprung fully grown from the barricades. The chief Communist party paper, *Scinteia*, ("the Spark") became *Adevarul*, ("the Truth") which was the name of a pre-WW II Romanian paper from the time when there was actually some truth in the Romanian newspapers. Numerous other provincial *Sparks* changed into *Truths* or *Libertys*. Many *Tribunes* also ceased to exist, and turned into *Forums* or *Dialogs*. *En lieu* of LONG LIVE CEAUŞESCU, the headlines now said LONG LIVE THE NATIONAL SALVATION FRONT

These prompt name changes telegraphed to the reading public that a) a revolution had occurred and b) everything begins anew after the revolution. The staff wishes to inform its esteemed readers that it has been forced to collaborate with the regime until now, but now that the revolution has come it is free to show true editorial colors which are—and had been all along—revolutionary, i.e., correct.

But *România Literară*, by continuing the traditional numbering, typeface, and most of its columns, conveys another message: Romanian literature, as practiced in the pages of this literary journal, has nothing to apologize for. No radical rupture has occurred in its pages between Romanian literature before and after the revolution. If it had been forced to collaborate it did so minimally, and perversely, in such a way that collaboration became defiance. *RL* was always subversive.

Looking over the provisional editorial board I find names associated, if not with out-and-out-dissidence, then with integrity and quality: Nicolae Manolescu, Octavian Paler, Alexandru Paleologu, Andrei Plesu. Nicolae Manolescu is Romania's foremost literary critic. The others are, to various degrees, dissidents of the regime's last hours. In Ceauşescu's Romania, the best writers were automatically dissidents, not because they made any overt political gestures but because they *did not*. In his last years Ceauşescu was no longer content with the perfunctory hosannas of his court poets: he demanded praise from everybody. He understood declared opponents but was tormented by silence.

In the upper left corner in the space usually reserved for a quote from the Maximum Leader, is a brief telephone interview with Eugène Ionesco. "Have courage and faith in God," Ionesco tells Romanian writers, "I'm happy that you're free. . . . I am convinced that only now it will be possible to express the true Romanian culture." These are the words of Eugène Ionesco the longtime Maximum Leader of Romanian writers, the very Anti-Maximum Leader Maximum Leader. Ionesco's first book, a volume of critical essays published in the 1930s, was called *No*. It was an attack on all Romanian literature before himself. Shortly after Ionesco's emphatic *No*, a larger and more brutal "No" instituted a permanent denial of past Romanian literature. The "No" of the Communists created a vacuum they attempted to fill with the so-called "doctrine of socialist-realism," a writing prescription that nobody took seriously, and then dismissed entirely after 1965. The "No" of the Communists was a mirage, but it constituted the first parenthesis that encompasses Romanian literature from 1946 until the December 1989 revolution. Ionesco's statement is thus the second parenthesis, the one that encloses the period, and closes the chapter.

But what is Ionesco saying? One the first words out of his mouth is "God." Consider the fact that Ionesco's column is replacing Ceaușescu's column. Forbidden by his ideology to utter the name of "God," the former Maximum Leader must have often felt keenly the vacuum where the Supreme Being could have been enlisted to his side, particularly since everyone in Romania could and did mention God casually, profanely or reverentially on a great many occasions. It must have given many people a great deal of satisfaction to be able to say "God" while knowing full well that their Maximum Leader could not. He lacked the legitimacy that even the most formulaic appeal to the deity gives most noncommunists. No such problem for Ionesco, who hates Communists, and whose rhinoceros, sometimes thought of as fascists, are really more like Communists, according to their author, and are thus known to most Romanians. For many years now Ionesco's symbolic rhinos were well known in Romania by even the most ordinary citizens.

After mentioning God Ionesco goes on to deny the very raison d'être of the journal's careful attempt—through numbering—to establish the unbroken continuity of Romanian culture. *"Only now,"* he says, "it will be possible to express the true Romanian culture." Once more, Ionesco is saying "no" to Romanian literature, the same literature *România Literară* is saying "yes" to by continuing with volume and issue number.

"All right," you might say. "Ionesco is on the telephone! He doesn't mean "only from now on," he means "now that you're free, you can say what you want," which is, to his mind, the only genuine practice. Literature can only be practiced in freedom. It is an important moment, a religious one: Ionesco, the exile, is given the center stage of his country for the first time since he left. A French writer of Romanian origin, he is Romania's greatest dissident because he has said "no" not just to the Communists but to all of Romanian culture. He has even abandoned the language. In other words, the most deliberate "yes," that of numbering, places the most deliberate "no" at its very center. If Ionesco the essential exile has come home, then it is time for *all* writers to come home, especially those writers who have never left, who had been in the most terrible exile of all, the inner exile of censorship. Ionesco reassures them not only because he is famous, French, and has "God" on his side, but because his very view of the human condition is one of estrangement. The exile leads the natives home through his profound belief in the absurdity of the world.

To the elite of Romanian writers who comprise the staff of the journal, the practice of literature is now at a perverse crossroads. Having wrested some spiritual freedom out of political un-freedom, they are not yet certain what the sudden lack of censorship might mean. The new freedom might be a new oppression, something that needs to be praised, a modality antithetical to people who've made a practice of refraining. What if they become paralyzed? What if they indeed need the censor the way nonbelievers need God?

Below Ionesco on the front page there is a column entitled "Never Again!" After a few moving phrases dedicated to the martyrs of the revolution (this is also, incidentally, the "heroic" issue of *RL*) the anxiety of writing freely rages. It is an ontological anxiety that questions not only the disappearance of the enemy but the nature of it. "We must begin," writes the editorial staff, "with an examination of our conscience. We must have the strength to look within. We must assume not only collective but also individual responsibility." The point here is that everyone collaborated in some way with the dictatorship, or it wouldn't have been possible. This isn't just an intellectual agony. A drunk man on the train from Timisoara to Bucharest on December 28 kept waving a bottle around the compartment mumbling: "We are all guilty! We are all guilty!" A friend kept trying to shush him, not because he thought the man was wrong but because it was embarrassing—in front of foreigners. "We would probably need," the editorial continues, "completely new typographical characters so that this editorial will cease to resemble even superficially those which for the past fifteen years have occupied this space. It was an occasional compromise that the powers knew how to make permanent. It is true that we had little choice. . . . [had we not compromised] we would have lost all possibility of communicating to our readers a certain critical spirit, in semiclandestine conditions, capable of maintaining the authentic values of our literature. . . ." A little further on, we read that, "writing has its own morality which ought not to be violated. . . . Just as there were those who profited from the dictatorship, there will be those who will profit from liberty. . . ."

Wishing for "completely new typographical characters" is revealing. In the nineteenth century, Transylvanian Latinists fought Slavophiles over typographical characters. When they won, they began officially writing Romanian in Latin characters instead of the Church Slavonic used until then. When the Soviets occupied Romania in 1945, the battle over letters had been long won but there was still a skirmish over the spelling of the country itself. The Soviets insisted that it be spelled with *i*—a Slavic character— to prove that Romania had enough Slav in it to justify occupation. Romanian nationalists—placated and then openly encouraged by Ceauşescu—kept and then changed *i* to *a*. Around this hatted *a* revolves the Romanians' claim to Latinity and to Europe.

If a new notation were possible, a new beginning would too, a beginning without the censor, a literature in liberty. A wish for "purification,"—a word much bandied about presently—haunts the literati, and not only them. Religious metaphors are everywhere. What *România Literară* calls "those who will profit from liberty," my friends called *de-azi de dimineaţă*, or "born this morning." We watched on television how officials one after another of the old regime declared their loyalty to the revolution. They had been born that morning, purified, completely different, free. One of my high school chums in Sibiu told me that my books—which I'd sent him over the years without a response—had been proudly displayed in his house. "Yeah," said his wife, "under the linen at the back of the closet." Her honesty was even more interesting in view of the professional tragedy she was undergoing: she had just finished her doctoral thesis on the revolution of 1848, and had been scheduled to defend it in January. Alas, it was riddled with quotations from Nicolae and Elena Ceauşescu. It began, in fact, with a long thought by Elena. "Now what do I do?" my friend's wife lamented. "It's already bound and typed!"

When I visited the Writers' Union, which is the official publisher of *România Literară*, the revolution was being loudly improvised by a number of writers going in and out of Mircea Dinescu's office. Dinescu, under house arrest until December 22, had announced the downfall of the Ceauşescus on television.

Ana Blandiana, one of Romania's best-known poets was there, complaining of the large numbers of Ceauşescu loyalists—Securitate—who were walking about unmolested. Dinescu was screaming on the telephone at the new culture minister that, yes, the Writers' Union was going to publish not one but three financially independent newspapers. After he hung up he made a face and asked: "Did I do the right thing? What does it take to publish a newspaper anyway?" I made him a list: typewriters, typesetters, computers, paper, pencils, desks . . . Dinescu then said, "We are making you a member of the Writers' Union!" Blandiana asked me to interview myself for *România Literară*, and then scribbled a number of questions in pale ink on a napkin. I still have it, but I have no idea what she wrote on there.

A poem by Dinescu is on the front page of this *RL*. "Haplea," the character of Dinescu's poem, is a destructive folk demon who is clearly Ceauşescu. Haplea breathlessly swallows church bells and lays waste the land with his "mechanical tongue." The poem laments the fate of the Wallachian land which since time began has been subject to destruction by anyone who passes through it. After three autumns, the poet warns, the windows will fall off your Wallachian house, and various barbarians will trample on your garden. Leading them will be our own Haplea, who is a traitor as well as a tyrant. "Haplea" is a beautiful, untranslatable poem, reminiscent of Ion Barbu's hermetic dialect poems. The list of barbarians is a litany of made-up words: "vin cumanii si pecenegii/si gugumanii si viceregii/si-n fruntea ostii saltind buricu/ Haplea al nostru cu polonicu."

Haplea is now gone. But isn't Haplea what happens to Romanians over and over? Lamenting an absurd history is Dinescu's, and much of Romanian poetry's, chief theme. Changing from lament to celebration would seem to call for a whole new kind of poet. And a new language. And a new beginning. And all those new things have already been done, under coercion, by Communists. The censor saw to it that they were done right, i.e, that nobody complained. Freedom, to be sure, is freedom to complain, and that is why, when the early ecstatic fog clears—it has pretty much cleared at the date of this writing, June 25, 1990, giving way to a soot-blackened sky of nouveau terror and *ancien* misery—the greatest chorus of complaints ever heard will issue unimpeded from Romanian—and other Eastern/Central Europeans—*culturati*, thereby opening a true critical path into the future.

Last time I saw Dinescu's signature was under a translation of a poem by Hans Magnus Enzensberger. Translation, in all its modes, will be the dominant postrevolutionary practice until new forms of lament are found. For Dinescu, at the moment, translation from the page to the political stage. For others, translation from who they were into who they are going to be. Whenever there is a before and an after, translation becomes the chief mode. I predict an explosion of translation in postrevolutionary Romania that will devour everything we write, even as I read it. In the period between the two World Wars, Romania had a literary flowering based in part on a voracious appetite for the outside world. After being shut in for forty-five years, a similar explosion is in the making. But in addition to being a natural desire to rejoin the world, translation will also be self-therapy.

On page two of *RL*, on the left-hand corner, there is a terribly interesting feature called "A Review of Reviews," or a "Digest of Journals." Quoted here are passages from various new (or renamed) Romanian journals. But under each passage, in bold type, there are comments by the linotypist who set the text. We are told in a footnote that "The interpolated text belongs to linotypist Gh. Popa, and we retained it." Most of the quotes are emotional homages to the dead martyrs of the revolution, and most of linotypist Popa's comments are supportive. For instance, "The new generation is the sacrificial flower from which the new Romania was born." Linotypist Popa notes: "A new Romania was born!" But in one case, quotation and linotypist are at odds. "Each one of our gestures should continue the supreme gestures of those who fell for the existence with dignity of the Romanian nation," reads the quote. Linotypist Popa adds a slogan from the revolution: *Ole, ole, ceauşescu nu mai e!* "Olé, olé, no more ceauşescu!" He spells "ceauşescu" with lowercase *c*, and adds: "As one printer oppressed by the monster, I beg you, do not ever write his name again with a capital letter in your review. . . ."

This plea actually gained support in the next week or so, and several newspapers, following the suggestion of linotypist Popa, began spelling "ceauşescu" with lowercase. Once more, the nation was embroiled in a dispute over a single letter. ("Lettrisme," I would like to remind you, the poetic movement based on the importance of single letters, was founded by Isidore Isou, a Romanian Jew. Of course, he founded it in France in French like any proper Romanian radical.) Eventually, cooler heads prevailed by pointing out that by making "ceauşescu" a lowercase noun his monstrosity would actually become smaller than it was. Hidden in linotypist Popa's proposal, however, was another suggestion, namely that by clearly marking the devil in this startling manner everyone else would be absolved from guilt and responsibility. To this day, most Romanian commentators still blame only Ceauşescu for the terrible years of the dictatorship. They forget that when he came to power he was a clone of the former Communist dictator, Gheorghiu-Dej. They forget also that he didn't rule alone. It would be infinitely more poignant if all the people who feel that they had collaborated in the gruesome drama of those years would begin to spell their own names with lowercase, in an act of orthographic humility that would be the Romanian Orthodox equivalent of the Catholic "Mea Culpa" the Polish Church was able to provide in the confessional for Poles under similar circumstances.

Under the heading "Life and Literature," is reproduced the important "Motion of the Provisional Committee of the National Salvation Front on the Editorial System." The committee, composed of many editors, calls for abolishing the so-called "Cultural Council," which had dictated editorial policy; the abolishing of censorship in all forms; the depoliticization and de-ideologization of editorial activities; the development of new editorial plans corresponding to the true needs and necessities of Romanian culture; the reprint of all the books rejected by censorship; autonomy. This motion is followed by the election of various provisional committees, composed for the most part of former dissidents and writers known for their integrity.

This particular action, together with the numerous laws and decrees passed in the first week after the revolution, are bound to alter profoundly the course of Romanian culture. Here is a good argument for the swift and decisive course of the Romanian revolution, against the superficial charge—often made in the West—that power simply passed from one Communist junta to another. (Or, as a French paper put it, "The most expensive personnel change in history.") The existence of provisional decrees and new names does not guarantee their implementation, but Haplea is decisively gone.

The last page of *România Literară* contains an interview with the French philosopher André Glucksman, who came to Bucharest on December 25, 1989. "Why are you in Romania?" asked Gabriel Liiceanu, the interviewer. "Because something I never believed possible happened here, namely the almost instantaneous collapse of a structure I have criticized in nearly a dozen books."

It's a funny answer. Glucksman has come to witness something in his books. He is a Westerner, and an outsider, but a hint of this kind of self-absorbtion can be spotted also in the genuinely happy pronouncements of the various Romanian writers here.

The sudden freedom of writing without the enemy has not paralyzed them, but has set in motion, rather, a radical doubt about "authenticity" in a future where the tests of it are as yet quite unimaginable. If anything, the sudden lack of an enemy has opened the dammed-up rivers of talk in everyone. When we interviewed citizens on the streets of Bucharest in January, we literally couldn't stop them from talking.

The problem of writing without an enemy may not be at all one of not knowing how or what to write, but one of maintaining enough silence for what is called "authentic" to be heard. If in Ceauşescu's "golden age," critics were needed to give definition to the whispers barely heard in the general silence, in postrevolutionary Romania their job might be to lower the decibels so that something might come through. Critics and writers—the meeting of which is *România Literară*'s strong suit—cannot divorce each other yet. When and if they do they will become like us here in the West where writers say things and critics say things but never to or about each other—and when a revolution of some sort occurs they go over there to see something in their own books—and to be interviewed on the last page of the first *România Literară* where writing has no enemy but all the writing is about the recently departed enemy. "Only now," said Ionesco. . . . Maybe so. Only Ionesco knows for sure.

How My Secret Twin
Saved Me

OVER THE YEARS I'VE HAD MY BRUSHES WITH
Hollywood. Someone making a vampire picture once called me
to quiz me about the density of vampires in Transylvania, where
I was born. I advised him on it (there are ten per acre) and begged
him to hire a Romanian to get the accent right. The picture came
out and the vampires spoke a mixture of Brooklyn and studied
Lugosi. So much for authenticity. Next time I saw my country,
Romania, was on TV when Joan Collins from "Dynasty" went
to a part of Romania called Moldavia, a fact announced by the
word "Moldavia" flashing across the screen. It looked suspiciously
like the orange groves of San Berdoo. A group of Moldavians
dressed like Libyan terrorists left over from the terrorist-movie-of-
the-week whisked Joan across the Moldavian-San Berdoo border.

That was the last I heard officially from Hollywood until the
dramatic Romanian revolution of 1989. In December of that
year our television sets relayed to us the most extraordinary
images of a country in the grip of a popular revolution. Immense
crowds calling for an end to dictatorship . . . the flight of dictator
Ceauşescu and wife in a helicopter as students begin burning their
books in the central square . . . the first firefights of the army with
Ceauşescu's dreaded Securitate . . . hundreds of young
people shot by snipers, their bodies displayed to the cameras . . .
the holey Romanian flag fluttering over army tanks, while young
soldiers fraternize with the revolutionary crowds . . . the battle
for the television station . . . On and on they went, these fabulous
images of an insurrection that seemed to spell a dramatic closure

to the collapse of communism in Eastern and Central Europe. And there were the horror stories: the torture rooms hidden in tunnels that honeycombed the major cities, the poisoned waters, the Ceauşescus' alleged vampirism, the murder of the children on the steps of the Timisoara cathedral, the madonna and child . . . It all became indelibly printed in our minds.

On Christmas Day 1989 the Ceauşescus were executed by a hastily assembled execution squad. The next day I left for Romania. I arrived in Bucharest two days later via the first train to enter Romania, the Orient Express from Budapest, Hungary. I had not seen my native country in twenty-five years. I reported on the fighting and the exaltation for National Public Radio and ABC News. But even as I was reporting, the stories from Romania became complicated and mysterious. No one was sure who had been firing on the unarmed demonstrators. The original body counts of sixty thousand dead were downscaled considerably. . . . to less than one thousand . . . there was evidence that the massacre of children in Timisoara never happened, in spite of the videotape we saw. . . . the water in Sibiu was never poisoned. . . . the "madonna and child" image was fake. . . .

In the months that followed the mysteries deepened. The men in power turned out to be secretly connected in a plot that went some way back. In June I went back for my twenty-fifth high school reunion in Sibiu, Transylvania. This was a "reunion" between quotation marks much like the "revolution" of 1989. A few of my old friends took charge of me for the duration of our "reunion." They had grown substantial, these friends, in every sense of the word. Most of them had gotten on well under the dictatorship. They owned houses, cars, farms. There was no dearth of food and drink. We spent two weeks steeped in brandy and sentimentality arguing fiercely about politics, while seeing now and then brief flashes of the thin boys we used to be a quarter of a century before. The oddest thing was that I did not recognize some of these "schoolmates" at all. I was sure the entire time that this was the fault of my overtaxed memory, but I am beginning to have my doubts. If you can fake a whole "revolution" in front of people why not a "reunion?" Fabricating memories was a Securitate specialty. This return was as strange as the first, and I decided to write a book. This book, entitled *The Hole in the Flag* was published and, of course, Hollywood called.

One particularly enthusiastic producer wanted to use all the details in my book as background for a love story between two war-weary *American* journalists. "Didn't they already make that? *The Year of Living Dangerously?*" I asked. "Precisely!" was the enthusiastic answer.

The next call came from a movie-of-the-week producer who had a similar romance in mind, painted on the ravaged romantic background. "If we can't have young lovers," she said, "how about a broken family reunited after decades?" I declined. And I also declined the third proposition, which was only partly more serious because it involved asking Costa-Gavras to direct the film. I declined this one because Costa-Gavras—even if somehow he was interested—was not the man for the job. He painted things in broad strokes and this Romanian business had ambiguities that called for an immensely complicated and perverse vision.

I was beginning to get very worried. There was absolutely no reason why these good people had any need of my book to make their movies. All the images of Romania in December were in the public domain. They could trivialize, twist and remake them to their mercenary hearts' content. They could put in love stories, AIDS babies and vampires, and have everyone speaking with Southern accents. There was no one to stop them. I prayed to the gods of history (nasty creatures, incidentally) to spare Romania from the fate of, let's say, India, as seen in *Gandhi*.

And then, a miracle happened. In the basement of the Plaza Hotel in New York where my publisher put me to publicize my book, a movie was playing. It was called *Requiem for Dominic*. It had been made by an Austrian resident, a Romanian-German named Robert Dornhelm, who was exactly my age. Using documentary footage as well as his own work, shot in Romania in March 1991, Dornhelm tells the ambiguous story of the Romanian events through a friendship between two men who had not seen each other for twenty years. It is a dark drama, loaded with all the creepy intensity of those times and it is . . . my book. It is *exactly* the movie I would have liked made from my book. "Thank you, ye gods!" I said, with only the merest twinge of regret. (Having to do with now never getting that expensive hot tub in Colorado.)

And thank you, Robert, my secret twin and ally, for thwarting (at least temporarily) the forces of conventionalism.

Black Water: Some Thoughts on The Fountain by Yuri Mamin

ROMANIAN REALITY WAS A CLONE OF SOVIET REAL-
ity for four decades. We lived in the same apartment building,
spoke the same artificial pseudo-languages and were seized by the
same profound sense of the absurd. We all lived in Soviet director
Yuri Mamin's building, and are all going down in it and with it.
In that sense, Mamin's metaphor of a communal apartment house
in Moscow is big enough to accommodate all of us now grubbing
in the ruins of the Grand Experiment. *The Fountain*, made in
1988, is a communal metaphor about community in several of
its guises: pre-community (the nomad tribe), faux-community
(several of these, corresponding to Soviet leaders), and finally,
post-community (which resembles Marx's "primitive communism" whence a supposedly rational communism was going to
arise—and did: into faux-community.) Of all of these, only the
nomad community makes any sense because its life is based on
ecological necessity, i.e., water.

There was a pure spring tended by an Orthodox monk at a
hermitage in the woods in the mountains in Transylvania when
I went there in July 1990. The monk looked 1,000 years old
and he'd written in old-fashioned script on a yellowing piece of
cardboard tacked over the spring: GOD'S WATER, DRINK AND BE
BLESSED. The guy who took me there was an old high school
buddy of mine who was secretly paying to have the fountain
restored. Secretly, because he was the regional communist party

secretary. His secret was his way of saving his soul. In his official capacity he would have had to order the fountain shut. In Yuri Mamin's film, the stupid truck drivers who destroy the entire ecology of the desert community by blowing up its water are not ideologues. They are just in a hurry and they are greedy. By the time they show up (in the waning hours of bolshevism), the ideological source of their greed and carelessness has been completely obscured. They have no souls, leave alone a plan for saving them. Nobody orders them to do anything. They are the perfect embodiment of the "new Soviet man," a creature without tribal memory, without respect, shortsighted and shallow.

All trouble begins with shutting down the fountain of one's beginnings. The ecology of survival is based on the wise management of memory and necessity. Without the fountain, the old man loses his raison d'être. He still has his values, however, and when he inserts them into the communal apartment building of the big city where he gets control of the community's water he acts accordingly. In the end he does re-create a tribe through his management of water, but it's a sad and ridiculous tribe of urban dwellers who know very little about tribal living. In the end also, Yuri Mamin's parable seems to sadly conclude that only a strong, authoritarian stupidity taken to its most extreme logical denouement can make a community out of people de-communized by communists.

All the right-wingers have whiskers. These are Stalin's whiskers, and there is an essay somewhere on the hair of communism. (Now, I'm told there is a film). From Stalin's downward-pointing yet somehow oddly-comforting mustaches to the sideburns and mops of early bolsheviks to Gorbachev's smooth bald surfaces, there is a gradual loss of hair. As communism began to wane, the heroic hair of the early years was replaced by baldness (boldness by baldness) until we arrived in the defoliated present of glasnost— Gorbachev, the cleanest-shaven man in Russian history. He was like the earth around industrial sites where all the grass is gone, burnt out by five-year plan after five-year plan.

This wasteland teems with bankrupt word-slingers, from the small party fry with their shopworn slogans to the poets waxing grandly under the toxic moon. (Mamin does to poets in *The Fountain* what Milan Kundera does to them in his novel *Life is Elsewhere*: holds them responsible for romanticizing terror while ridiculing them.) Shouting in mutually incomprehensible tongues at each other, these people have had even the most basic communal tool removed: verbal communication. I remember looking at the front page of *Scînteia*—the Romanian *Pravda*—and falling asleep. It was pure narcolepsy. All those recurring meaningless words held us hypnotized for years. But in the mid-sixties we believed that the words of the poets might wake us. No such palliative in Mamin's world. The party official who complains about the lack of a wall gazette and fresh slogans seems quaintly old-fashioned, a throwback to the Brezhnev utopia which was: communism is correct slogans! Quaint too is the veteran who goes to turn his family in all decked out in medals. No one is listening any longer. The old man praying to Mecca in front of the refrigerator (because it faces East) makes as much sense as the theater director holding forth on how "the theatre is a fascist place." All the buzzwords, "Mecca," "fascism," etc., have lost meaning. In their stead arises a kind of buzz, an *ur*-paste of language.

One of the film's major metaphors, translation, is exquisitely layered. From the woman translating to the old man and to her family, to the Hemingway on the wall as the elder wails away on his banjo, to the mutually incomprehensible yet perfectly comprehensible and ultimately incomprehensible speeches and slogans, we are witnessing a spectacular failure of communication, a Babel beyond Babel. As the roof, the attic and the basement are collapsing, the humans within are mirroring the collapse in language. The last reality seems to be unreality. "You'll never see yourself on TV because you're such an idiot," is one of the film's grand lines. It epitomizes and probably prophesizes the future in that the last place of certainty left is television, the screen of pure illusion. Yuri Mamin pays an ironic and backhanded self-conscious hommage to his own medium here. There is no salvation in this parable and fairy tale either, he tells us. *Enivrez-vous*. The voting scene shuts the last door left, the possibility that people used to mind-numbing conformism can learn how to be free. Not a chance. I remember endless Pioneer and Komsomol meetings where we voted just like that.

Mamin's vision is unsparing. The sad Icarus with his violin is a figure of ridicule and pathos, not redeemed even by talent. He is an urban angel, the attempt of a discredited, romantic, sentimental imagination to escape with cardboard wings from the nightmare without end of the communal apartment house.

I lived in one of those when I was a kid. One day my mother and I came back to our one-room apartment with private kitchen and bathroom and found a large family of twelve peasants in our kitchen. Their clothes hung drying from clotheslines strung all over our stove, and our tiny icebox was stuffed with indescribable lumps of lard. They had broken down the door with an ax and moved in armed with a paper from the local secretariat. I was attacked by one of their kids and I started swearing at him in my best city-kid slick manner. His father took out his belt and tried to whip me. My mother screamed. When the old man in *The Fountain* whips the city kid, he does so in all innocence. Our peasant was shocked that my mother objected to his whipping; he thought that she should be grateful. Eventually, she pulled in all her markers and traded all we had so that we could move into a new place. It was half the size of our miniscule old one but it was *private*. In fact, the old man and his values are not idealized by Mamin: his tribal customs are seen with the same unsentimental, unsparing eye as the rest of the sorry crew. The feeble attempts made to conform to his whims—which call for men and women to eat in separate rooms, for instance—are met with well-deserved derision.

The black water in the tub is almost too painfully apposite to the clean spring of the beginning, but here I see something of Mamin's fluency with the language of fairy-tale metaphor and, perhaps, some of his facility. Nonetheless the gritty reality of that black water is so familiar it transcends metaphor. We too had a bathtub where the water was always blood red when it wasn't brown. No amount of complaining or fiddling with the pipes ever pointed out the reason. For fifteen years or so my mother and I washed in bloody mud. We got used to it.

The apartment house is, of course, a microcosm of the glasnost Soviet Union, and it is very thorough. The worshipers of the ancient poet gathered about the dried-flower shrine of his verses are familiar to me as well. The nostalgic keepers of the Russian Orthodox flame have an equivalent in the nationalist poetry society in my hometown whose meetings I occasionally attended. They were worshiping Octavian Goga, a fiery and facile Transylvanian who was a minister of state under two right-wing regimes. They read his poetry in a cold-water flat, were driven to rapture reciting his verses and ended up singing nationalist songs fueled by *tzuica*—our vodka—until they passed out. I used to steal books from the apartment because they were not available elsewhere. Today the Romanian national sentimentalists are having a huge revival just like Pamyat in Russia. The irony of the poet-worshipers defending the rotten wallpaper where the poet once scribbled is accurate: these remnants of the old are worshipers of wallpaper, only the forms have remained. There is nothing here but the general rot of the apartment and society's walls under the poetic paper. (At the same time one should never underestimate the force of sentiment: fascism is stupid and mostly sentimental!)

The new capitalists aren't spared by Yuri Mamin either. The flower-grower squatter is trying to create a market economy all by himself, but he is dependent on the water controlled by the insane old man. What's more, he's trying to grow *flowers*, the most pathetically tender product imaginable, dependent on vagaries of so many kinds it is a doomed enterprise no matter how much luck he has. Again, the metaphor is flawless. You can no more grow flowers in a waterless cold apartment building than you can fly off the building accompanied by bad sentimental music. All of these people are cursed by what they have collectively made and they cannot pull away individually from the shithouse. Either they all go down together or they go down together. There is no exit—and this movie is probably late communism's master existentialist critique. Interestingly enough, Mamin thinks like a social determinist, he is clearly educated by Marxism. The collectivity communism sought to create *is* a collectivity, but it is hell. Utopia turns out to be hell and it is a collective hell. In that sense, there is a kind of endearing familiarity—affection almost—for this world which is the only one Mamin says these people will ever know. We have made our bed and now we lie in it.

A careful reader of this film will find himself in a garden of interpretive delights. The language of the film is fluent, metaphorically rich and relentless. I am only noting here things that echo for me personally. Romania, a similarly mad apartment building, was not as decayed in 1965 when I left the country. Mr. Mamin brings me up to date on how deeply the shabby edifice has rotted since then.

The new tribalism of post-glasnost society is the very opposite of materialism. All materials have disappeared. The material world has thinned out completely, resources have been squandered, any semblance of ecological balance between people and environment is gone. In the end even the guys holding up the roof cannot be fooled into helping what's obviously doomed. They are bribed with alcohol to do so, and in terms of currency vodka has replaced slogans. The slogans themselves, in one of the most touching motifs in the movie, have been retired and aren't even good for patching holes. In fact, every hopeful illusion—or even hopeful language—in Mamin's world is utterly false. We are in the presence of a new and intensified radical doubt.

Robert Duvall as Stalin: The True End of Communism

THE END OF STATE COMMUNISM DIDN'T COME when Gorbachev dismantled the USSR, or when Yeltsin introduced the market economy. It truly and finally came when Robert Duvall, a great actor but an American right-winger down to the tips of his cowboy boots, got to play Stalin on HBO. The first time around, history is a tragedy. The second time it's Hollywood. And this *particular* time, it's Hollywood with a vengeance.

Bobby Duvall, as he likes to be called, lives on a horse farm in a beautiful part of Virginia. It's an aristocratic landscape of rolling hills with genteel estates set comfortably in them. You can glimpse large Georgian and Victorian mansions through ornate gates sporting lions or vaguely English coats of arms. Horses that look good enough to model in paintings graze dreamily in the dark-green grass. It smells like honeysuckle and, but for the engine of my car, it is preternaturally quiet. Not far from the Duvall farm is a tiny town, if you can call it that. It consists of a small grocery store with two gas pumps. The store is an old-fashioned wooden house from the end of the last century that smells nostalgically of mysterious barrels, candies, sodas and medicines. It doubles as the post office. Virginia hams in cloth sacks hang from the ceiling. The ancient behind the counter eyes me suspiciously when I ask for directions. "I'm not one of those autograph nuts," I assure him. "But you might be a vegetarian," he says with a grin. Now, that's funny. How did he know? He gives me directions nonetheless.

The Duvall house is a pretty brick building at the end of a

curving driveway. It's not a monstrous mansion of the kind one associates with Hollywood stars. On the contrary, it's a homey, down-to-earth place. A boy on a tractor is mowing the grass on a field next to it. Mr. Duvall, in jeans and boots, opens the door himself. Here is the Godfather's *consiglieri*, Tom Hagen, Lieutenant Colonel Kilgore from *Apocalypse Now*, Frank Burns from *M.A.S.H.*, MacSledge from *Tender Mercies*, the Great Santini, Jesse James, any number of outlaws, President Eisenhower and now *Stalin*—and he's an unaffected, country-easy fellow with a disarming smile. But knowing what a good actor he is, I try not to let his charming simplicity disarm me. After all, I had heard that he doesn't particularly like interviewers. He can be gruff, uncooperative and distant. He's also famous for his temper on the set, where he has often clashed with directors and producers over the direction of a film or the interpretation of a role.

I have my own agenda. Although I admire the actor, I'm not here to put another feather in his well-feathered publicity cap. I'm here because of Stalin. I was born in Romania just after World War II, moments after the victorious powers represented by Roosevelt, Churchill and Stalin divided the world. The part of it that I was born in fell into Stalin's hands and nothing was ever the same. Our little history-whipped but spirited and rich country became, in the next forty-five years, an impoverished, unhappy and sinister land. Stalin was the daemon of my childhood but he was also, because I didn't know any better, a kind of father to me. His smiling portrait towered over the central square of my hometown. In all my schoolbooks, there were pictures of him surrounded by adoring children. I didn't have a father of my own, so Stalin's paternal presence was comforting. I had his portrait in a small tin frame by my bedside table. I sometimes recited a prayer that my grandmother had taught me: "Our Father who art in Heaven/Blessed be Thy name . . ." It was addressed to Stalin. The day he died, in 1953, everyone cried, me most of all. But when I came home from school I overheard my stepfather talking with another man. The man said, "I'm glad the SOB is dead!," and my stepfather said, "Amen." That was that. I could never look on

Stalin innocently again, especially after I heard the details of his criminal life, but an irrational child's affection for the protective mustache under which I fell asleep persists to this day.

"Some of the people he put in prison even wept. . . . he had that kind of hold," Duvall said, when I told him that story.

The sixty-one-year-old actor grew up during World War II, mostly in Virginia. His father, Rear Admiral William Howard Duvall, was stationed in the North Atlantic during the war. His son does not remember Stalin being much discussed around the table. He does remember being a newspaper delivery boy when he was ten, and being told by his dispatcher:"I suppose we have to worry about Stalin next." When Stalin died, Bobby Duvall was in college. One of his school pals said: "A great man passed."

"I realize what a stupid thing it is now, how he pulled the wool over so many people's eyes," adds Duvall.

"Pulling the wool over people's eyes" concerns the actor, who thinks that people, especially in his business, are politically, if not existentially, deluded. "I was on the phone with Alan Parker last night and he said, 'Anybody who's sensible is to the left.' That's so predictable. There are so many of these old leftists in En-gland. . . . I said to the girl who was playing the lead, 'You don't know what it's like to live under Stalin,' and she said, 'Try living under Margaret Tha-atcher.' "

Duvall draws out "Tha-atcher" with just the right touch of English accent, and he's made a whole picture with that one extra vowel. I can see the naive girl, the old English leftists, and the fact, somehow, that leftism is a kind of continental affectation. Duvall himself is an American, and planted squarely on earth. He tells me that instead of *Stalin*, the HBO film that will soon be released, he almost made another, called *The Inner Circle*, shot by former Soviet film maker Andrei Konchalovski in the Kremlin, with an Italian cast. "The Italians are all Communists. . . . and telling the Russians they ought to keep this going . . . they are Gucci Communists. In fact, I think, really, the film we made was the Gucci left of Hollywood. . . . we made a film about the Gucci left of Russia. . . . that's what it boiled down to . . . Lenin and all those guys, they lived like kings!" He holds the exclamation point in the air for a brief moment, then laughs.

I get the impression that Duvall is not so much interested in politics as he is in being the devil's advocate. He delights on being on the "wrong side" from the fashionable liberalism of show business. "The left is very active in this country now," he pronounces gravely, but when I say, "The left of what? Who can tell what's left or right any more?" he backs down a little, to what he knows for sure, "That's what show business is in this country," and adds, "everything out of my mouth on the set around these English was politically incorrect."

Robert Duvall has played an extraordinary range of roles, mostly villains, but different as Jesse James and Eisenhower must have been, they were all Americans. He is an essentially American actor who understands and loves the contradictions and dimensions of the American character. I tell him that I'm surprised that he has chosen to play Stalin, a man incomprehensible even to his fellow Russians. He readily admits that we know very little about Stalin, the man. Most of what we know comes from books and newsreels that reveal little of what went on "beyond the scenes." What's more, Stalin was "by design, an enigmatical guy. He studied to be muted, Georgian, oriental, mysterious. . . . he worked at that. He wasn't flamboyant like Castro, or Hitler. . . . there is nothing on him."

When Duvall says "muted" and "there is nothing on him," I begin to understand why he chose the role. Duvall's best portrayals, people like Colonel Kilgore in *Apocalypse Now*, who goes surfing in the middle of a war, or Tom Hagen in *The Godfather*, who holds the delicate balance of power between the passions of his Sicilian bosses, are intense individuals whose actions suggest great inner tensions, hidden depths. He is an actor capable of creating the impression that there is a great deal of mysterious, unspoken life behind a simple gesture or a single phrase. His best villains are "muted" and "mysterious," which raises them above the level of one-dimensional cartoons. There being "nothing" on Stalin must have actually helped Duvall to portray him. What's more, he gives even the worst of them some human quality. But was there anything likable about Stalin?

Duvall admits that "it was hard within the confines of the script" to find anything good about Stalin. "We had to try to find that . . . the final scene before he dies, I made up a half a scene. . . . I found out a Georgian saying that means 'My time has come,' so I have him predicting his own death. I don't know if that happened in history, but like someone said, 'We're telling history how it happened or . . . how it could have happened.' You got to make up something. You got to find something to make up within what you feel is real because there is not much there to go by. There is even a theory that he killed his own wife. . . . but even if she committed suicide over him that's bad enough. If it's true, you'd have no movie. . . . it would be just one color after another, black, black, black. . . . I tried to find the human side at the end where he would relate to his dead wife's picture. . . . in reality, he cut out little figures and made a shrine out of her. . . . he got a bit senile. I used that scene to show that he had human feelings. . . ."

Duvall's acting is clearly more important than his politics. Finding Stalin's "human feelings" doesn't exactly fit in with his hardline conservatism. He has once said that in order to understand roles he studies similar people by "hanging around their memories." I ask him if among the many petty tyrants he has encountered in his professional life, people like movie directors and producers, he has ever met anyone resembling Stalin.

"No," Duvall says quickly, "but whenever in doubt I fall back on rhythms of speech. . . . I had a Ukrainian landlord. . . . an old ballet master in my past . . . but I really don't know. I felt that each day when I went to work if I came up with too much preconception about this guy I would head myself off at the pass, so I would go there with fear and trembling, not knowing what I was going to do." During the filming, the cultural attaché from Canada told him: "I admire what you're doing because you, an American playing a Russian, you're finding history in your own way, day by day."

It occurs to me that Stalin himself must have worked at being Stalin pretty much the way Duvall did. He must have gone to work at the Kremlin day by day, in fear and trembling, not knowing exactly what he was going to do. The insane policies that killed millions of Russians during successive waves of terror often have the feeling of being improvised rather than the result of rational thought. Yet, once they were decided, these decisions were implemented with murderous fury by his henchmen. Stalin himself was an improviser, whose bad decisions ruined his country and held the whole world hostage to fear. It's too bad that he was a tyrant, not an actor. Interestingly enough, like many other dictators, Stalin started out with some artistic pretensions. He wrote poetry. So did Castro, Ho Chi Minh, and Mao. Hitler wanted to be a painter. Duvall has actually hit on something essential. But he goes a lot farther.

"I did a movie on Gypsies once," he says, (*Angelo My Love*, which he produced, edited and directed) "and there is nothing really noble about Gypsies. There are noble things about the Jewish people, but there might not be anything noble about Gypsies. They are both wandering people, similar to Jewish people but Jewish people have made interesting contributions. . . . so I thought that Stalin was like a Gypsy, in a way. . . . anything goes . . . ."

Well, that's Duvall, in a nutshell. There are as many contradictions in that statement as there are in any of the roles he played. *Angelo My Love* is a wonderful, sensitive movie about Gypsies, played by real Gypsies with whom Duvall made friends in New York. Passion and compassion spill out of his actors. One would think that their director loves them, yet he does not find them "noble." He's not overly fond of Jewish people, either, in spite of finding them "noble."

"There was this Jewish guy on Ted Koppel who was with the Rosenbergs," he tells me, "he worked for them (the Russians) helping with armaments, and now he's got his American passport back." He has no doubt that the Rosenbergs were guilty. What's more, he quotes a Chicago columnist that "there were a lot of

Communists in Hollywood before McCarthy. They say that before that if you *weren't* a Communist you couldn't get hired." But he quickly notes that this "may not be true . . . McCarthyism was too much." In fact, he refused to play McCarthy when he was offered the part. Still, "according to the *New York Times*"—Duvall is careful to always list his sources as if he himself were somewhat skeptical, but what can you do when there are such authoritative sources!—"there are closet conservatives in Hollywood who are afraid to speak out." After a pause, he adds: "On the other hand, that's the most hypocritical town in the world. How many studio heads are blacks? It's the most capitalistic society out there!" But like the man of contradictions and complexity that he is, Duvall also notes that L.A. is a comfy town. "I like the weather. . . . I wouldn't mind living there if a judge sentenced me and said, 'You have to live there.' It's OK, I guess."

Now, I'm not sure if Duvall is either a right-wing nut or a closet Communist. He likes taking things a bit far down the right-wing fantasy road, despite the disclaimers. Some of his ultraright fare sounds straight out of David Duke territory, the Jewish-Communist conspiracy, and all that. David Duke himself comes up for consideration on the matter of his facelifts. Duvall has met Louisiana's Governor Edwards, and he asks: "How many facelifts do you think Edwards had?" In other words, Duke's facelifts may be unfairly held against him.

We get back to Stalin via the Jews. "He hated Jews, but he kept guys like Kaganovich in his circle." Stalin's anti-Semitism was as virulent as Hitler's, but it never attained the kind of "scientific" insanity that took root in the German's sick brain. After remarking that he found nothing to identify with in Stalin, Duvall confesses to some sympathy nonetheless. "He was like a street guy. . . . a common criminal. A hillbilly, on the one hand, a street con on the other. Country smarts plus street smarts could make a hell of a leader." Stalin reminds him of a couple of toughs he knew, and of an Argentine Basque tango dancer hoodlum. "The intelligentsia hated him."

There is a hint here of Duvall's own feelings in the matter. He likes street hoods, hillbillies and Argentine criminals. He's not sure about intellectuals. For one thing, they are all "leftists." I had been under the impression that Duvall had been well treated by film critics and by academics. But he remembers negative criticism in detail, and can quote a bad review with great indignation. "That prick, pardon my language, had the nerve to say. . . ," and then he quotes verbatim what the prick said.

I ask him about the feelings he had while working in the Kremlin, sitting where Stalin sat, walking where he walked. "We had carte blanche up to a point. Sometimes they wouldn't let us in because you had to pay a guy off. In certain scenes I thought we'd be better off in Culver City doing the sound, but in others you had to be there. In one way it was great, in others there was too much red tape, but in the end it adds up because . . . *there it is*! You can't buy that." On the other hand, (there is always another hand with Duvall, a prestidigitator's magic hand) he found Moscow a "joyless place. It's a very strange country; There are no perks. You don't just sit out and have coffee for an evening, have a drink on a hot night. . . . everything is tough. Tough city." He quotes his director, Ivan Pashcke, a Czech émigré, saying that blacks in this country didn't have it as tough as the people over there because here "they can always get in a car and move," but there "they are stuck."

The political commentary that underlies all of Robert Duvall's stories is quite a mix. I get the feeling at times that he is playing someone else, George C. Scott maybe, or John Wayne. But where George C. Scott's political opinions are the genuinely frenzied hallucinations of an extreme right-winger, and John Wayne's politics were carefully tailored to fit his Reaganism, Robert Duvall's attempts are rather ambiguous. It occurs to me that he may be too much of a nice guy to buy a whole political line. And despite his tough guy pose, he is genuinely interested in human beings, an interest that, fortunately, makes pathetic nonsense out of most ideology. He reminds me of a typical uncle at a family picnic, intent on shocking his younger, milder relatives.

In fact, he does not prejudge anyone, not even Stalin. He even tried to summon him forth one night, at his dacha, but the dictator didn't come. It must have been quite a scene though, Duvall with his hands in the air, summoning the ghost of communism. It should have been in the movie.

Duvall also interviewed one of Stalin's head bodyguards, and asked him: "If someday you have to meet Jesus Christ, how are you going to face him?" He said, "How do you know I believe in Jesus?" Duvall then asked him who he thought was the greatest man in the world, and he said: "Lenin. Maybe Stalin." "The guy obviously believed," Duvall says half-admiringly, "he now runs a music school where all they play is Stalin music for the accordion."

Duvall himself was raised a Christian Scientist, and it is said that he doesn't drink or smoke. I can believe it. At sixty-one he is trim, fit, an excellent tennis player and a horse rider. When he tells me that he played a set with Ilie Nastase, the Romanian champion, he can't help adding: "I heard that all Romanians and Italians cheat at tennis." You hear the darndest things in some circles. Christian Scientists don't believe in doctors and, curiously enough, Stalin also hated doctors because he thought that they were going to poison him. I wonder if he felt some sympathy with the dictator on that score, but I refrain from asking.

I ask him instead what he thinks about the astonishing speed with which history becomes movies these days. Duvall says: "We capitalize on the hardships of the world." I realize then that I may be in the presence of someone as irreverent as a Gypsy. Nothing is quite sacred, not even his own profession. Duvall is a consummate devil's advocate, a joyously populist malcontent. His sense of humor is anecdotal, and there is always a little unspoken moral hanging at the end of his tales. His stories are a bit like a preacher's parables, but this may be because of the interview format. I can imagine Robert Duvall telling some truly wild stories to his intimates. But the preacher figure is real to him. He has been struggling to obtain financing for a movie about a preacher in Louisiana. The way he tells it, it's a wonderful story about a man with a past who finds redemption. But it isn't so much the story that sounds good, as his genuine affection for the place and for its people. He thinks that the South has been misrepresented in movies "from *Gone with the Wind* on down." But he's not a chauvinist. When it comes to directors, he says: "Better a talented guy from Australia than a hack from Dallas." Most American directors are better with cities. When it comes to the South, Duvall thinks that "they ought to be met at the Mason-Dixon line with shotguns."

Duvall's politics may in fact be less an ideology than an attempt to be like the people he loves (and loves to play): Southern rednecks, patriots, outlaws, cowboys, officers in peacetime. Without meaning to, he has probably transformed Stalin into some kind of American archetype, some kind of Western villain with a touch of Al Capone. But that may not be the case: Duvall's energy and versatility are amazing. Last year, in addition to being Stalin, he was Pulitzer in *Newsies*, he was in a Camus-based film with William Hurt and Raul Julia, and was a detective in an upcoming commercial film. He would rather not theorize about where all this abundance comes from. But his timing is right. *Stalin* was shot in Moscow shortly after the failed coup against Gorbachev. The cast was jumpy. They knew that the coup leaders had ordered "forty thousand pairs of handcuffs and eight concentration camps." The movie company had "eighty thousand dollars stashed aside in case we had to get out fast."

This sort of excitement may be unsettling to a novice, but to Duvall, who endured the Philippine jungle under Francis Ford Coppola during the making of *Apocalypse Now*, it's just his work. In fact, in spite of the apparently agitated tone of his conservative politics, he seems like a man well at ease inside himself. When he isn't working, which is not often, he likes to ride his horses. He looks forward to spending time with his jumping horses this summer.

I don't know how much I learned about Stalin, but I did learn quite a bit about Robert Duvall. He is a hardworking movie actor who has reached the kind of plateau that can all too easily become a bully pulpit. Duvall does sometimes appear to be using it just that way, but his sense of humor and his glaring (and proudly acknowledged) contradictions save him in the nick of time. When he says, "I don't identify with the left in this country. I sensed that something was B.S. with it," you hear something folksy and quite unthreatening. On the other hand, as Duvall might say, it may not be all that benign. If a truly far-right party ever came to power in the U.S., such pronouncements may take on a darker hue. Remember, Stalin wrote poetry.

Driving back, I admired once more the genteel, unself-conscious wealth nestled in the green rolling hills of Virginia. I could have been ages and thousands of miles away from the torment of American cities, and the din of politics. On the other hand, we were less than an hour from Dulles Airport near Washington, D.C. Big planes were taking off for all parts of the globe right in the neighborhood.

IV *Culture and Sport*

*Throughout the ages The Monks stored
the secret of bread, I warmed ambition
along a tropical memory, and The Nuns
kept a finger on the clitoris. The
ability to eat at a Mexican Restaurant
in the company of my enlightened associates is deeply indebted to these
circumstances, and I offer this poem
in place of cigars and brandy. Now,
about that girl by the parking meter.*
JEFFREY MILLER

What tended to be most desperately lacking
took its value above all from what grew in
such profusion nearby.
ANDRE BRETON

The Word Made Trivial

I WAS WEIGHING MY TWO PASSIONS, THE ONE FOR prehistorical/antihistorical/atemporal/sacred speech, and the one for the strictly contemporary/the newest/hottest hippest stuff happening, trying to decide which one consumes me more. The first would be poetry in some sacerdotal but also demiurgic sense, the other drama because it implies an audience. The first would be literature also, the second journalism. Or, if you prefer, art and life. The two are not different except in sound: one hums (transports) like a wave (fairy-tale hypnosis), the other alerts like an alarm (gossip, traffic lights). There was a time there, for a few hundred lousy years, when poetry and drama (life and art) went their separate ways, but that was the Age of Darkness which I have just decided to terminate. Many Ages of Darkness (i.e., formal separation) have been ended by poets proclaiming them over. Some of these proclaimers: Blake, Rimbaud, Whitman, Ginsberg.

Certain things are apparent: contemporary poets long to reestablish direct contact with an audience, a contact that was once broken. There is an international, anarchistic, antistate, antiestablishment movement that seeks more than an esthetic experience. It is utopian and revolutionary. It is also theatrical, dramatic and formally innovative. At its formal borders the distinctions are reestablished. Then the long darkness begins again. On the one hand: "The whole world's a stage," and Antonin Artaud's idea of theatre as a cultural experience that includes non-Western ritual dance, shamanistic practice, sacred medicine and totemism. On the other, the structural defense of tender materials moved between their specific weights like chemical compounds. An audience grows into the new combinations. Are both possible? Simultaneously? Yes, briefly, when the Darkness gives way. The light, sure enough, obscures everything soon enough. "We are hidden in the light." (Lucian Blaga)

Persuasions and esthetics come into play either for or against a direct assault on the audience. For, they attempt to destroy "literary distance" either through use of new technologies (tape recorders, synthesizers), chanting, voice projection, mixture of voice, paint, dance. They try to restore poetry to oral tradition and to song, where it all began. Against the audience, it's *art pour l'art*, as if it can be anything else. In the dark, art is at its most artistic. Class is at work: the mob wants *some* entertainment, even from their poets. The upper class demands only one thing: difference from the mob. The best class defense is obscurity. The specific obscurity of the Age of Darkness is the bourgeois demand for boundaries. Art in our fin de siècle is fully in the business of boundary-making, barrier-erecting. But then come the Terminators, with proletarian bulldozers.

In the beginning, a long time ago, once upon a time, when there was no time, when time was an idea whose time hadn't come, when apple trees made cherries, and the sky was so close you walked on it, and fleas brought us the news, not newspapers, and horses were so small that you could hold them in the palm of your hand, there was only one story in the world, and everyone told a little piece of it. Also about then the only kind of writing there was was the tracks of birds and animals on the ground, the writing of clouds moved by wind, the intricate arabesque script of the sea writing on the land. People used to read this writing, which was the writing of the gods containing instructions for the proper telling of tales and the performance of them. And when they read it, they said it. This was an uninterrupted kind of writing that ran through everyone and everything under the name of *Logos*, but not everyone and everybody could tell the story. Unfortunately, this function was reserved for the poets or shamans who were set apart by the gift of travel between reality and dream. Storytelling was the same as medicine because words in those days didn't just tell, they also cured. The storytellers told the founding epics of the world which were also the medicine that made the world right by negotiating between humans and spirits. All the sacred acts of the gods before the beginning of time were recalled in this telling. These acts, if carefully repeated, would keep everyone within the circle of the sacred which was the circle of the story. No harm would come to them from history. History, to the storyteller, was an assault of the chaotic and trivial forces of disruption into the story. It was an attack on memory. A Fall into Time. The Fall, repeated by every myth, is a Fall into History, Time—a place where all is trivial and disconnected.

From those beginnings to our day, through literature, we begin to perceive a gradual loss of meaning, a trivialization of poetic speech, a fall from the sacred into the profane which parallels the fall of tribal societies from cosmic/ritual existence into history. The vulgarization (trivialization) of poetic speech corresponds to a loss of memory and a loss of collective sense. We forget and we fragment. Differentiation and individuation operate at all levels: the once-medicinal word becomes a cry for help. From a tower somewhere in the fragmented body the word-yielder is imprisoned by the word. *L'art pour l'art* shrinks the world to the size of the increasingly shrinking cell. The world gets smaller, the words more empty.

In the *Art of Memory*, Frances Yates speaks about the medieval Gnostic memory systems, and suggests that we today have no memory at all. She dates this loss from the moment that we put our faith in books and other devices for storing knowledge. Before the advent of writing, everything we knew had to be connected to everything else in the world, in order for it to stay in us and make sense. Knowledge was inconceivable without wisdom, that is, without those general principles that put the things we knew in the perspective of all the other things we knew. But with the advent of books, we began to trust large portions of our knowledge to them, in the belief that we could always look it up later. But what we really did was to make holes in the synthetic harmony of our being. We began to marginalize ourselves, put ourselves out of the center of our world to the periphery. WE CEDED THE CENTER TO THE BOOKS. The process has gone on inexorably and rapidly from Gutenberg on to the point where we now store graphically or electronically everything we know about the world, living in blissful ignorance with our presumed access to the buttons. (Store replaces story.) Our brains have never been as far from our fingertips as they are now. The knowledge at our fingertips is mechanical, disconnected, dead, *sans souffle*, not animated by the living understanding of our place in the universe.

Now it has been the jobs of poets to keep the Logos alive, a task made increasingly difficult by the depersonalization of the poetic act and the power of central media to colonize, vulgarize and destroy speech. The electronic media is seeking to replace our human nervous system with its own. TV fathers, mothers and children are more real to us than our own families. Under these circumstances, the poet's job, never an easy one at any time, is truly heroic. He/she has to fight not only against the eroding of connective tissue and the trivialization of language and thought, but also against its own cooptation and contamination. As the written depends only on the written, a poet finds himself inside a vicious circle of substance sucking by his own products' products. What was once living becomes Naturalism, Realism, Surrealism, Modernism, Postmodernism, etc. The speaker diminishes and the speech becomes all. But this is not the same speech as the sacred speech of the beginning: this is the even speech of machines, not the unpredictable story of the gods. This is speech turned upon its own devices, speech about speech. The cosmogonic myth and the fairy tale are replaced by the novel and television. The ritual-sacred utterance becomes a bourgeois commercial proposition feeding endlessly on the demands of a self-perpetuating market that is not an audience but, precisely, a market. Who reads? Who watches? The reader and the viewer have been replaced by the Spectator. Utterly different creatures these three: they vary physically. The body of the Spectator is a strategic map for the deployment of cultural products. The reader and the viewer used to touch. That is now forbidden: art is produced for the sake of production, which is to say for the sake of storage. It is made to be noted, credited and put in résumés, not to be actually read. In fact its message may be exactly the opposite: *NOLE ME TANGERE, DO NOT READ ME. Art pour l'art* is *art contre l'homme.*

The poet today is like Scheherazade: he must tell a story each night in order not to die. If he dies, the sacred, the Logos, dies with him. He has to fight for his imagination, he has to please the king, and he has to guard against falling asleep. He has to fight for himself and for the world. And he has to chronicle, much as it hurts, the diminution of the sacred. To destroy and conserve are minute by minute activities.

How do we set the world right again? The poet Jerome Rothenberg, for instance, thinks that we must begin with a radical reconsideration of our Western views. Poetry on this continent did not begin with Whitman, or even with Ebenezer Cook, but with the Mayans' sacred epic *Popl Vuh*, with the Iroquois' *Great Tree of Peace*, with the Hopis' *Song of the Humpbacked Flute Player*, the Aztec *Definitions* in the Florentine Codex, the Mandan *Tree of History*, the Dakota *Good Winter Count*, Black Elks' *Spirit Song*. We must also rethink our literary canon, to include the poets of the blues, where perhaps the greatest American poetry can be found. How can we have a poetry anthology that does not include Robert Johnson or Lightnin' Hopkins or Muddy Waters?

The task of restoring to the poet the special place in the world that was always his, so that he in turn can restore all of us to the center when he reconnects us to the Logos, isn't just anthological and historical, however. If anything, it is not historical or anthological or canon-making. The idea is not to make a new canon to replace the old one, but rather to create a conspiracy of inclusion, in which the human voice is allowed to roam freely. We must recuperate all the speech excluded by literature, slang, technobabble, mass-hypnotic advertisement and insanity (these by taking them out of context), Spanglish, Frenglish, all the bits and flotsam of collective, oral idiom. And we must be strictly contemporary, totally hip, right on top of things. "The business of art," said Gertrude Stein, "is to live in the actual present, that is the complete actual present, and to completely express that complete actual present." Now how can you do that from a box, whether it be a book or postmodernism? Or Ezra Pound: "It is dawn at Jerusalem while midnight hovers above the Pillars of Hercules. All ages are contemporaneous in the mind." Which is to say the strictly contemporary is the same as the sacred. They both bypass history to reunite in the oral telling.

Beginning of fairy tales/myths as time machines to put one in separate time/space. Separate speech (sacred) removes the universe from mortality to separate time/space. (The only way we have of being immortal). Sacred speech is immortality. Poetry and immortality spoken in the same breath since forever. Trivial speech is instantaneity, oblivion.

The paradox of our increasing power to project and our decreasing sense of utterance is well illustrated by the decrease in the emphasis of readings by modern poets. Between the first recording ever made, Lord Alfred Tennyson reading *The Charge of the Light Brigade*, and the latest poet reading without emphasis a long work of almost total "nonreferential" language, stretches a loss of memory as great as our libraries.

The Unsurveyed Arts,
the Unsurveyable Artist

THE ARTIST AND THE ART ADMINISTRATOR'S points of view are not the same. They seemingly have much in common, but on close examination they reveal their differences. I am going to present the artist's side of the story, emphasizing the places where they intersect the administrator's.

Everyone is being surveyed to death. The survey has, in fact, replaced intelligent discussion in this country. Between the survey and the public opinion poll we have a perfectly ignorant public that doesn't really know what to think; it knows only how to answer yes or no or maybe to questions that have been formulated a priori by people with vested interests. The questions asked by surveys contain their own answers insofar that they are the linguistic and ideological formulations of the people who ask the questions. Given the choices, there is little room for the honest opinions of the individuals.

What happens to the honest opinions of the individuals? They either fail to come to light or they are shared with friends and neighbors. If they fail to come to light, it is because we are too lazy and too harassed to invent the language in which to express unsurveyable opinions. If we do formulate opinions that are unsolicited and share them with our friends, we create, in effect, an underground knowledge, an unsurveyed territory. In my opinion, we have both in this country. Failed articulations are by far the majority. People who have been cut off at the pass by the articulations of surveys and public opinion polls become passive consumers of entertainment, veritable black holes into which the entertainment media and the political lobbies pour all their products. The majority of our public is a black hole kept open and excited by entertainment and policymakers along lines defined in public opinion surveys. These are the people who at an increasing rate consume television and clichés, making those markets swell and grow to the fantastic dimensions we see today.

In the arts, the survey presents additional problems. In order for the artist to function he or she must exist outside surveys. To the arts administrator, on the other hand, the survey is absolutely essential. How else determine the size of an audience, the need of a community? How else obtain the facts and figures that are needed to make a case for the allocation of funds?

Artists are duty-bound by their art to sabotage the familiar in order to express an unsurveyed and, hopefully, unsurveyable personal reality. Their very existence is predicated on the as-yet unexpressed and, hopefully, inexpressible. Let's call these high-minded creatures "real artists." For every "real artist" however, there are a hundred not-so-ambitious ones, whom I will call "mainstream." Mainstream artists are not really fakes, they are merely people apt at what they do, apt at gauging public taste and quite cognizant of surveys. They may even be real artists who found the demands of their art too severe and so took the easy way out. There is a real dilemma for the arts administrator here, a dilemma that goes way beyond taste. Who should receive public support? Those who go against the grain of surveys or those who please the people?

Take writers, for instance. The mainstream writer in America is a small-time producer in a cottage industry where things are done pretty much as they were for several centuries, notwithstanding a few modern frills like the computer and Federal Express. The mainstream writer is basically interested in getting paid for entertaining readers trained by our schools, publishing houses, and cultural and educational programming. These readers know what to expect from writers who know what they expect. Both reader and writer have been well surveyed: they know (or think they know) what they want from each other. The writer feeds the black hole of the reader with the words called for by his survey makers. Certain kinds of these writers do not need public support: genre writers of romances, Westerns, mysteries, television and movie writers. But others do, particularly university-trained workshop writers.

The workshop writers masquerade as non-mainstream writers but that's only an illusion; they simply cater to the surveyed needs of a different class of consumers, namely academic institutions. Notice I said "consumers," not "readers," because, properly speaking, these workshop writers do not have readers: they produce their materials for résumé-building in order to fill the self-generating slots of a growing bureaucracy. These writers do not even read other members of their résumé-building subgroup. Their books exist only to become lines in a résumé, and would, in fact, suffer terribly from being read. Many of their books carry an injunction written in visible-invisible ink right over the copyright notice: DO NOT READ THIS BOOK. These writers are institutional insiders disguised as outsiders.

The mainstream can be described as a creation of two markets: the regular, capitalistic one that we all love and know, and the bureaucratic-institutional one which differs from the first in that the product has only symbolic value. The regular market, which produces the bewildering variety of pop sameness that we see in bookstores and supermarkets, is superior to the institutional market because its products are used. Use-value is superior to symbolic value.

Now let's take a look at some other writing, writing that stays underground and unsurveyed, writing that, I believe, is the job of art organizations to ferret out and support. This writing sometimes goes by the name "avant-garde," but that is a somewhat problematic term. Let's just say that this is a species of writing that resists instant gratification, writing that challenges the reader's assumptions, that raises more questions than it answers. It is writing that sometimes looks unusual because it does not follow the conventions of grammar and spacing that make other writing accessible. It is writing that deals in an unusual way with taboo questions of morality, society and the status quo in general. The less it yields to the conventional modes of reading the more interesting it is. It is sometimes crude, sometimes overly sophisticated. It can be found in very small magazines, even Xerox zines. It can be heard in off-the-wall reading places, in bars or in living rooms. It is writing that does have a readership and an audience, no matter how small, but it is a voluntary and passionate audience, unlike academic writing, which has an obligatory audience. Funding and supporting this kind of writing is imperative because it is the only one operating outside the numbing forces of the two markets I mentioned. (There is a false paradox involved here, namely that funding and recognizing this kind of writing might bring it to the surface and incorporate it into the mainstream. Even if that is occasionally the case, its continued vitality and regenerating ability guarantee its continuation. Failure by success is more of a problem for mainstream writers.)

The problems of marketing and funding are even more acute in the visual arts. Unlike books, works of visual art are mostly one of a kind and they demand a different approach, one in which ideas and ideology are of utmost importance. You are no doubt familiar with the main arguments raging in the art world today. The problem of art-critical language, the existence of an art market for investment purposes, the rapid succession of styles, fads and fashions. I recently saw the work of Mark Pauline and John Reiss of the SRL (Science Research Laboratories) in San Francisco, work that seems to me to define very clearly the possibilities and situation of art today. SRL researches, designs and creates fantastic machines, and then puts on big spectacles involving these machines. The machines themselves are useless in the conventional sense of that term, since they exist solely to dance, hiss, crash, self-destruct, catch fire and act out their whimsical designs. The SRL spectacles often have a polemical and provocative edge, as when they make fun of their audiences. In Amsterdam, one of the machines was an insane windmill that attacked itself, while in Copenhagen a giant cow filled with sour milk was busted open by a mechanical worm straight out of *Dune*. In some sense, the

SRL spectacles looked very much like Hollywood's special-effects department gone haywire, but the show made profound sense.

We have arrived at a certain stage of technological sophistication where we are much too good at what we do in relation to the ends to which we put our machines. How many perfect F-15s and other fancy killing machinery can we produce? The uses to which we put our machines are medieval, ideas that make sense no longer. Combat, the way it was once understood, is no longer noble. Yoking everyone to the insane producer-consumer cycle of an endlessly greedy and increasingly faster capitalism makes no sense either. If machines were originally meant to give us more "leisure time," they have in fact done the exact opposite. We are on a treadmill. And yet, there is no doubt that, as a species, and as a nation, we very much enjoy inventing and creating machines. Americans have a mechanical genius that is wonderful. What better use then for this spirit than the creation and invention of machines for play? If all hints of usefulness and conventional reference were removed from these machines—and that includes the conventional references of Hollywood movies where fantastic machines are used in the service of inane morality stories—we could have our cake and eat it too. SRL works as a collective, incidentally, where everyone is paid the same, whether they are designers, scavengers or operators. They are a model for a technological society that won't go away. They exemplify, it seems to me, the social dimensions and possibilities of an art that isn't merely decorative, academic or made-to-sell.

Folk art exists on the same level. Folk artists, like the SRL, make beautiful things to express the things that the entertainment industry cannot provide. They are fountains of unsurveyed art. The religious motifs of much of this art testify to the stubborn impulse to say something while playing. In art, maintaining the idea of play against the assaults of the surveying world of art criticism and the art market is a difficult business. Again, as a funder, I would look only at art that is insistently playful and disdainfully serious.

"Staying unsurveyed," to coin a new phrase for the genuinely artistic state of being, is to adopt an adversary stance to the received ideas and clichés of the mass media, as well as to the fabrications of critics seeking to build pretty little cages of words around the work of art. This does not preclude, of course, playing with those clichés and those critical notions as much as one likes.

I have not, until now, used the word "subversive" on purpose, because I did not want to cloud the issues in areas where there is plenty of confusion already. I do so now, in order to make a couple of small distinctions. Writing and art must be subversive, which is to say they need to be true to the "unsurveyed spirit," true, that is, to their innate playfulness and individual necessity. This is not a matter of "taste." The subversive quality of a work consists precisely in how much of a shock it is to one's ideas of "taste." The publishers of small, purposefully obscure and hard-to-read zines, produced deliberately cheaply and crudely, graffiti artists, and others, engage in direct art action meant to challenge current assumptions of "taste." Of course, "taste" changes quickly, and the mainstream is quite capable of absorbing yesterday's shocks and making them today's conventions. After all, the "historical avant-garde" is now an academic subject. Literature is not as yielding as art in this regard. I don't know of many zines that have become mass-market magazines, but graffiti artists, like Keith Haring, for instance, became big-time art businessmen when they joined their enemies. There is always this possibility for artists, which writers are luckily spared because they do not make unique, displayable objects that can be captured in the neat cone of an art-critical butterfly net. If I were an art administrator, I would look for artists who are in no danger of selling out, either because what they make self-destructs or because it doesn't fit anywhere. Writers I would fund on the basis of how unnerving it is to read them.

What is the intended audience of the "unsurveyed artist" and how can art administration conceive of it? Collection, distribution and publicity are integral to your job. My opinions on these subjects are as follows: I do not believe in permanent collections of art, i.e., museums. I believe in temporary collections that are continuously rotated, exchanged and renewed, while the art house itself should serve as a clearinghouse for artist information, performance space and publications. Distribution of funded projects should be an inventive business originated by the artists themselves, but if they do not want to distribute or publicize their work, that should be perfectly fine and they should not be required to do so. In fact, if they wish to destroy their work, they should feel perfectly free to do it, no matter how much money you put into the project. Likewise publicity. Artists and writers should have the right to refuse to have their work publicized, but if they wish to do so, you ought to help them in any way you can. I realize that documentation and publicity are the grease that makes the wheels of budgets roll, but there ought to be alternative ways of convincing legislators to appropriate funds, personal ones perhaps—things like "unpredictable dinner with an unsurveyed artist in his or her own lair," at their own risk. Unpredictability ought to be the major principle of enlightened art administration, a kind of Heisenbergian physics of uncertainty. What's more, people receiving the benefit of art should be made aware of the danger involved. For the art administrator there is a kind of masochism involved, because part of every true artist's job is to bite the hand that feeds it. On the other hand, it feels good to be bitten like that. In fact, there are few greater pleasures than to be well bitten.

Please wear gloves and give generously.

A Kind of Love

THERE ARE TWO KINDS OF LOVE I CAN THINK OF right off the bat. One kind is the kind I call Stat Love, which is the kind you study and discuss, the kind of love that thrives on facts and statistics. The sum total of what you know about the beloved is the beloved, except that there is always more to learn and more to know. If you're in Stat Love, you are her public defender, the messenger of her qualities, the trumpeter of her records, the fan of her history. She is the ideal, and you are the pest.

The other kind of love is the Roomy kind. You know little about her and want to know even less. You simply want to be in her presence, inhale her atmosphere, be in the room she creates around you, lose yourself, be entranced. Not only do you not know her stats, you don't even know yours any more. She has put you in a magic space-time, a place made possible only by exaltation. This is the kind of love I have for baseball, which is a good excuse for ignorance.

I saw my first game at Memorial Stadium in Baltimore in the spring of 1979. The Orioles were playing the Angels. I was much taken at the time with the literalism of sports headlines, and I was amused at the idea of birds fighting angels. I also liked bears squashing padres, and different-color socks going at it. As my friend Jeff Miller used to say: "Ouch, ouch go the little padres." Rodger Kamenetz, a friend of mine, took me and my son Lucian to this game and I didn't understand anything. Both Rodger and my son filled me in on fine points, but I couldn't tell who was scoring, when and what was happening. The sport went against any idea of ball games I ever had. The week after that week I went to a game all by myself. Rodger asked me what the score was. "Nothing to nothing," I said. He laughed. The score, plainly in the morning paper, had been 12 zip.

I was involved at the time in a struggle to get my citizenship, and I was having an epic battle with the immigration department. I had the weird feeling that I wouldn't get my citizenship until I learned baseball, and that's exactly what happened. The first game I went to and understood from start to finish was the Birds and the Tigers in the summer of 1981. The Tigers are another favorite of mine for various mythical reasons having to do with Detroit in 1967, and the delirium and riots of 1968. And as soon as I understood that game, something popped in me, the pod opened and the nouveau American I always was suddenly emerged. And of course, I got my citizenship, the Orioles won the pennant in a spectacular series where Eddie Murray hit a home run on the bottom of the ninth with the bases loaded, and at the citizenship party at my house my friends gave me a baseball signed by all of them in a little ceremony. The party lasted all night. I take that ball wherever I go; it's moved with me to Louisiana, where they don't even have major league baseball. There are Saints here, but they are football saints, not the same at all. With citizenship and a baseball signed by all my friends—my son has one signed by Sandy Koufax—I started to understand large tracts of American writing that had been closed to me until then. Things like Fielding Dawson's stories and the esthetics of the Black Mountain school of poetry and painting. The whole late fifties, early sixties art movements that established America as the leader in painting— abstract expressionism, pop art and the rest, were all secretly and not so secretly cornball attempts at a vision of America in a state of baseball.

Baseball is very literary. There are well-known writings on baseball, from Dawson to Malamud, but there is something else.

Both baseball and poetry begin in childhood. They are mirror images in a way. Baseball is the active form and poetry the contemplative. Now a poet like Edgar Allan Poe, whose grave is on the way to Memorial Stadium in Baltimore, wouldn't have liked baseball. He was an aristocrat who hated the masses; he preferred the night to the day. He loved silence and despised crowds. Which is ironic, because Baltimore's rough democracy did him in. He was killed by vote salesmen, hoods hired by the local pols. On the other hand, it isn't entirely inappropriate for this city to love both their poet and their baseball. There is a lyrical link between the two. When the cheers of the crowd carry on the wind and wash over his grave, Poe can dream that the crowd is cheering for him. He wouldn't be wrong. They are cheering a ball being set suddenly free, which is very much like a poem freed from its poet.

Poe isn't the only marker on the way to Memorial Stadium. There is also the place, near the Peabody Institute, where Freud first came when he came to America. The occasion was the founding of the American Psychonalytical Society. This too is significant. Freud, who said so much about everything, would have said wonderful things about baseball too. Speaking of Houdini, "the last great mother lover," E. L. Doctorow said that when Freud came to America, mother love died forever. I wonder if baseball, which is always mentioned in the same breath with mother and apple pie, could have withstood the force of *Herr Doktor*'s critique. Would apple pie? Probably. Freud would have taken to baseball the way he took to cocaine. Mid-European intellectuals have an *organ* for baseball.

Before I saw baseball, I never knew a sport where people didn't worry about the ball all the time. In soccer there is constant competition for the ball—the identity of the player is defined by his possession of the ball. He *is* when he is touching the ball.

In baseball there is a different relation between ball and players, and consequently, between game and spectators. The ball is allowed more personality, it is permitted distance. It is stalked rather than gang raped. It is also a dance between two men—a Spanish dance. It is a corrida, a bullfight. The pitcher is a toreador—he stands and acts like one—the batter is the charging bull. The ball is the toreador's life—issuing out of him as an eternal tease to the brute power of the bat. It is a battle between spirit and flesh, between two different kinds of cunning, a cultivated one and a natural one, between civilization and nature.

There is some evidence that baseball was brought to America by Romanians. Transylvanian shepherds play a primitive form of stick ball called *oina* that resembles baseball. Some Romanian officers visited Cooperstown and showed the natives. Even if *oina* isn't exactly baseball, there is a Latin connection. The many Spanish players that give the game its contemporary salsa may claim an Aztec lineage. The Aztecs too played something like baseball. Some of the major-league players of Central American origin instinctively combine the style of the corrida with the existential seriousness of the Aztec game—the ceremonial ball game. In the Aztec game of pelota the winning team was put to death. It was a great honor to be made into an instant god. The game was played with hips and knees only; you were not allowed to use hands or feet. There were two stone bases or goalposts, a large stone horseshoe and a parrot with a small hole in it, called a *pama*. The *hatcha*, or the court, sloped down between stone walls. The spectators were arrayed along the top. The game had cosmic and ritual significance, no doubt. In any case, it was serious, just as the corrida is serious. In modern baseball, that seriousness is a matter only of certain moments. The moment just before the pitch, for instance, when everything is in suspense. The world becomes very mysterious at that point.

I hear too that a ball pitched at a speed higher than fifty miles an hour cannot be seen. The last batter capable of seeing high-speed balls was Ted Williams, whose batting average in 1941 was over .400. So it is a truly mystical game. The batter has to know somehow where the ball is, and hit it before it gets there. A good batter can bat with his eyes closed, using the mystical sense. The high rate of failure with the bat would be unallowable in any other sport. Seven out of ten! A basketball player with that kind of failure rate would be inconceivable. Baseball's high rate of failure makes it a game of extraordinary tolerance. What's more, the players are arranged according to what might happen in the field. *Anything* might happen, except what *does* happen. So in addition to great tolerance for failure, baseball is a game of possibilities. That's the American ideal par excellence, it says so on Miss Liberty. Send me your failures, I'll make them possible.

There is something in the game that goes with the American landscape. Its essence is waiting, not rushing. There is a streak of patience, almost stoicism in it. Likewise the great prairies, the Western ranges. People rush across these, of course, but they find themselves overwhelmed. Even the fiercest gold rushers soon found themselves stilled, overwhelmed by the land. America has not yet been made human. The land is still the true power. The geology. Space, as Olson said, is the central fact of man in North America. Baseball has an understanding of American space. The lulls in the action, when the spectators can eat hot dogs or sushi, drink beer and converse, are large reprieves, islands of wonder. The whole cosmos can bear down in the pauses between action, and does. When the end of the world comes, whole stadiums will be spirited straight into the sky in the space between two pitches somewhere around the fourth inning in a steady, even game.

The language of the game is interesting. You can think of the pauses as caesuras, breaks between the lines. As a poem the game is composed of a number of short lines representing the pitches. The number of lines per batter form a stanza. Then there is a space. Sometimes the stanzas become breathless, rushing full paragraphs that build rapidly on each other until the poem-inning explodes. The poem lives for this sudden blossoming out of prosodic regularity. Should someone make a computer analysis of baseball prosody, I believe that they would come up with something close to the prosody of some great American lyrical epic, Whitman's *Leaves of Grass*, let's say, or Doc Williams's *Paterson*. Of course we could be surprised by its coming out like the *Popol Vuh*, the Mayan epic, or Bernal Diaz's *Conquest of Mexico*, or even *Don Quixote*. Prosody is funny. The game is definitely an epic though, formed of many lyrical moments dependent on silences for their effectiveness. An unfolding story punctuated by brief emotional swellings. Football is a pure narrative, a straight short story on the C&W theme of "How long can you hold on to something everyone wants?" Football is a linear short story that aims straight for narrative continuity and a thumping climax. Soccer is all lyricism without any relief from the intensity. The ball is oversexed, the players overexcited.

The sexuality of baseball is different. Both men and women like the game. Football is mostly a men's game, a straining against the massed flesh of the world to achieve a difficult penetration. It is direct and genital. Baseball is courtly, there is a lot of romancing of the ball in it, teasing, coyness, missed opportunities, ground gained and regained. The bat-penis is teased and teased by the ball-egg. The teasing is meant to elicit maximum potency, the batter's terrifying best that will send the ball out of the ballpark. Out of sight.

In this sense, the game is predominantly female. It is played on the body of a woman—the diamond—symbolic of the body of mother earth. The initiative belongs to the pitcher, who is the servant of the egg, the yielder of the tease. Like the toreador he is often so exaggeratedly macho that he is positively hieratic, impossible, artificial. He is a highly skilled drone, tending to the work of the queen. A palace minister who knows the ins and outs of his mistress's will. There is a direct and personal rivalry between him and the batter. Although they are both men, the batter represents only himself and his masculinity. The pitcher is responsible for the egg, and for the form of the game. The kinds of things pitchers sometimes do to batters, like hitting them with the ball, have to do with the frustration of being a hired hand—albeit a metaphysical one—facing a free man. In reality they are both doing the bidding of the feminine: one intimately, the other cosmically. Overtly and covertly. The overall plan is union: freeing the ball. Orgasm (scoring), of course, is the goal of all sports, but some sports have weak, attenuated orgasms—like golf (WASP orgasm), while others, like soccer, have demotic, indiscriminate slumgasms. Baseborgasm is soaring, dignified, serious, roomy. And there is time for a snack between the convulsions.

Baseball crowds are also different. They are summery, picnicky, beer soaked, light. Those gruesome rushes of collective aggression in football are missing. I love to sit, slightly high in the stands, letting the mood of the crowd flow through me when the home team is winning. In Romania, I was not allowed any communion with the masses. There, the division between guys with glasses and guys with muscles is unbreachable. There is nothing more terrifying than walking up the street as a postgame soccer crowd walks toward you when the home team lost the game. You have glasses, you are Jewish, you have on a lycée uniform, there is only one of you and the whole history of intellectual, class and racial persecution is about to bear down on you. The individual and the mass. All the alienated existentialism we provincial Eastern European Jews invented, along with modern literature, comes from that immense fear of seeing that crowd advance toward you. I realized that the reason I'd never gone to a baseball game before 1979 is that I abhor crowds. They scare me. When they stand up as one, tens of thousands of them, screaming, I thank God they are crying for a ball not for the blood of Jews. But the feeling is similar, and the adrenaline the same. What must it have been like to be a Jew disguised as a German at one of Hitler's rallies? I don't want to think about it. But my fears were allayed, if not totally put to rest. There were all kinds at the game: Jews, guys with glasses, housewives in shorts. Goodwill and hot dogs prevailed. Of course, there are warlike sections like the one Wild Bill

Hagy used to sit in, but those beer-bellied brutes just don't like suits. There is a big difference between that and muddled politics. I don't like suits either. One might make a case for the innocence of American political conventions and the ignorance of the electorate as corollaries of baseball, but that would be stretching it. Baseball is cornball all right, but it is not simple.

Am I Fit to Live?

A LOT OF WATER HAS FLOWN UNDER THE BRIDGE since the day my fourth grade phys ed teacher, Comrade Fiddle, wrote on the board *MENS SANA IN CORPORE SANO*. That's Latin for "a healthy mind in a healthy body." This was the classical ideal as it had come down to us from our Roman ancestors. Romania, or rather Transylvania, where I grew up, prided itself on its Latin roots and the classical heritage. The trouble was that Comrade Fiddle was far from classical. He was an obese tyrant whose idea of physical instruction was to exhaust us in meaningless runs around the gym, push-ups and military-style drills. He would line us up in our tattered shorts—it was a poor country, everyone improvised—and comment on our physical appearance. He called me "stick legs," because I was skinny, and later when I got glasses, he added "four eyes." I came to be known as "stick-legs-four-eyes," a monicker that delighted the more brutish members of the class, who lost no opportunity to poke me on the playground and demonstrate their physical prowess by knocking me down.

In truth, I was mostly *mens*, and I became convinced early on that the world divides into guys with muscles and guys with glasses, and the twain shall never meet. Consequently, I spent most of my time reading and ostentatiously carrying a huge book under my arm to flag my preference. When things got really rough I called on my stepbrother, who was an amateur boxer and a scrapper, and he beat up my enemies. He offered to teach me to defend myself but I haughtily declined. I spent the years of my early adolescence walking restlessly from one end of the town to another with my head in the clouds. I never ate anything because

I was never home, and my mother worked and didn't like to cook. When I got hungry I went to the farmers' market by the Cibin River and tasted cheeses, apples, pears and cherries under the pretext that I was shopping for my family. We also had coupons to eat at the printers' union cafeteria, but the food there was an invariable mess of gruel with bits of gristle on it, so I stayed away most of the time.

There was nothing fit about the people I grew up with, neither their minds nor their bodies. Among the many radical reforms the people of Eastern Europe and the Soviet Union will have to undertake will be the complete overhaul of their diets and of their bodies. You've never seen such masses of pasty slobs as now haunt the empty market stalls of those ghost countries. Fed on cheap carbs and boiled bones, it's no wonder that so few of them have enough energy to tend to their physiques. Jane Fonda recently took her aerobic message to the ex-Soviet Union and found thousands of people interested in . . . looking at her work out. The truth is that those countries are environmental and human disasters: the people are as despoiled and anemic as the landscape.

When I was growing up, in the late fifties and early sixties, working people followed sports, mostly soccer, not only because there was little else to do but also because sports scores were the only honest facts printed in the newspapers. Everything else was lies. Romania had as fine a slew of sports heroes as any communist country where athletes were used for propaganda abroad. We followed their doings with dutiful interest, but only soccer elicited passion. It was a kind of passion that makes me shudder to this day. I once walked up the wrong way toward an angry soccer mob after the home team lost. There I was, a skinny, bookish kid with glasses, carrying a poetry book, pure prey. I escaped the wrath of the mob by disappearing behind one of the huge medieval doors that opened opportunely as I passed by. Otherwise, I would have been dead meat. To the soccer crowds of those days I was a perfect representation of everything that was wrong with our world: an unathletic spindly scholar who would one day lord it over the honest folk who worked for a living.

I sometimes used the city swimming pool because I liked the solitude of swimming laps, but I quit going there when some of my classmates started hanging out. I was not consciously athletic but I was a great walker. I also nurtured the obscure desire to be immortal. Romania was renowned for a magic substance called Gerovital, synthesized by Dr. Ana Aslan. Dr. Aslan's drug and her clinic attracted thousands of rich old Westerners who wanted to live forever. These seekers after the fountain of youth may have also known that our fairy tales, particularly in Transylvania, were full of hints of special herbs and magical waters that gave eternal life. But they surely knew about our Dracula, whose vitality was world famous. Some of them must have reasoned that if Gerovital failed, drinking blood might not. I'm not sure what immortality has to do with fitness, except that everyone would like to be fit enough never to die. At least, I think so, when I see how strenuously my contemporaries are now cultivating their mortal coils.

I was pleasantly surprised when I came to the West to see gorgeously tanned, well-shaped giant individuals smiling at me from billboards advertising all kinds of delights, including liquor and cigarettes. These were special beings, however, not at all like the real inhabitants of Detroit among whom I found myself. People in Detroit had thick, well-fed Midwestern bodies originating for the most part in the pork-worshiping peasant villages of Eastern Europe and Germany. They were stouter and taller than most people I had known and I felt even skinnier among them than I had among undernourished Romanians. I lost two inches of height as soon as I disembarked in my new country. I had been of average weight in Europe but here, among the sturdy denizens of the New World, my averageness was reduced to shrimpiness. I was now a skinny-legs-four-eyes-shrimp.

When I moved to California in 1970, I became aware that many people here considered their bodies objects worthy of great attention, to the exclusion of everything else. In California, youth was being worshiped. Not any youth, but that golden mythological youth-body whose perfect smoothness dazzled the beaches. I saw perfectly golden youthful bodies engaged in aerobic exhibitionism before my eyes and I felt, once more, inadequate.

Thinking to derive some spiritual benefit as well as some muscle tone, I began a yoga class where the spiritual and the mental could be had for a single price. I quit the eating of meat and felt immediately and irrevocably superior. (Also, it was the cheapest way to eat since I didn't have any money.) I floated for a while on my cloud of light and brown rice, but I soon became disenchanted with the snail pace of my physical improvement. The pretzel-posture I assumed every morning was making me unaccountably dizzy.

I quit, and evolved a yoga of my own that consisted of four steps: 1) Walking, 2) Flirting, 3) Sex, 4) Self-flagellation. I followed these four steps rigorously every day over a period of several years. Walking had clear benefits: it stimulated the mind, it took me over and to interesting places, it gave my whole body a sense of purpose that made it one with the land; Flirting, while not strenuous, involved a great deal of energy and complete attention as I concentrated on communicating the entire vitality of my vibrant young body to a complete stranger sitting obliviously across from me at a coffee shop with a book of poetry in Sanskrit in her long, pale, piano-playing hands; when flirting successfully the body-involvement was extreme: every muscle worked subtly. Sex, a result of either successful flirtation or multideveloped fantasy, had the best aerobic benefits of all the steps in my program: it exercised the body even as it released negative energy into the void; it also invited a transcendental dimension into the repertoire of physical gestures, filling the muscles with meaning. Self-flagellation, which sometimes followed the energetic ecstasy of sex, was a form of drawing the body back from wherever sex had flung it in the wide and irrepressible universe; this gathering in had a slowing-down function, and while it sometimes hurt, it was necessary (and it was, for the most part, psychological; I never used whips!—like some people I know!)

I came out of the seventies very well fit. By this time a variety of fitness crazes had taken hold, some of which I found intriguing, while others seemed very weird to me. My mother sent me the first Jane Fonda workout tape as soon as it came out. I don't know why she did that. There was no reason for her to suspect that I wasn't taking care of myself: I was. But you know how mothers are: she envisioned me up all night having sex and doing drugs with the rest of my generation. I was, but I was also taking care of myself. Perhaps she thought that Jane Fonda would inspire in me a desire to make money. See, my mother wanted the tape to say, here is a woman with political views as weird as yours who is yet fit *and* rich. Mother may have also thought that a man would never get me to exercise. Well, the tape didn't do too much for me, and neither did Jane Fonda. Later, when I found out that she'd been a dedicated bulimic while I was following my four-step program, I became even more convinced of the superiority of my method.

I *did* start running, though. Ten years later. It was the eighties by now and certain things had changed both in the world and in me. The world had become a more dangerous place to flirt, for one thing. It was almost as dangerous to flirt as to hitchhike. You could be picked up by Jeffrey Dahmer, for instance. Or his female equivalent. Personally, I didn't have much sympathy for the newly cautious Republican Age, but I slowed down nevertheless. I was typing a lot more, at my desk, instead of migrating through cafés with my notebook and pen. I also got down to the business of family and children, a rather sedentary and food-centered activity. And to top it all off, I had to make a living, another (mostly) static endeavor.

Years passed this way, until I rose from my desk one day and noticed that I had swallowed my typewriter. I mean, there was a typewriter's equivalent of flesh protruding from my midriff. My children, who had grown quickly and actively, pointed to my Olivetti of flesh and giggled. That's how children are.

I started running around Audubon Park in New Orleans where I was now living. I refuse, I told myself, to get fat and look like a slob. (There was also an incipient bald spot on my head). I refused also to give in to the conventional wisdom which decrees that parents should begin to look like barrels at about the time their children turn into amphoras. Both my sons were athletic and fit and loved sports: they were both working toward karate black belts, played basketball, baseball and football. But they were also very good in school, and so they were true Americans, thank God! There was no division for them between muscles and glasses; they had both.

I ran for almost a month before I eliminated the flesh Olivetti completely. (I sold the mechanical one too, and bought a computer). A bad ankle put a premature end to my running, but I would have quit anyway. I was philosophically unsuited for running. Deep in me something warned me not to fool with a profound self-defense mechanism that decreed running to be an extremely serious response to Cossacks chassing you with whips. Running was written in my genes as the natural reaction to pogroms, anti-Semites, people in uniforms and peasants. It wouldn't do to trivialize it. Running for the sake of running instead of running *from* something was sacrilegious.

I spent the next few months looking for a new form of fitness. I stared into the well-lit windows of exercise places where well-heeled middle-class yuppies worked hard to shed enough calories to make Eastern Europeans rosy again. (I think that the total number of calories shed by Americans in one year equals the total amount of Third World intake). I also spent some time watching television for hints of fitness. The most interesting program was a Christian weight lifting class led by a televangelist who dedicated every barbell to Jesus. That wasn't really for me, though I did try some weight lifting at my local JCC where my sons liked to hang out. I sat dutifully under one of those weight machines lifting dozens of pounds with my hands and feet, in an order prescribed by a young guy who looked like Arnold Schwarzenegger. Everything hurt after these sessions so I gave them up too. I decided to carry twenty pounds of books at all times, instead.

While my physical fitness enthusiasms waxed and waned, I held steadfast to my diet, though, so I didn't get fat again. Since I'd been more or less a vegetarian ever since the days of my four-point program, I became an even more resolute one in my middle age. When I ate right the energy I expanded in the course of a day seemed to be sufficient. On days when I spent entirely too much time typing or reading, I tried dancing around the house with the dog. (Nobody else would dance with me). I returned also to the first point of my program, Walking. I have been fortunate enough to live in interesting places like San Francisco and New Orleans where the streets are alive and colorful. When I watch people and stare into windows I don't even feel that I'm walking. The truth of the matter is that I can walk miles and miles in cities (especially New York) without feeling the strain. I have also lived in the country where the air was good and the landscape beautiful, but I must confess—to my embarrassment—that flowers and rocks don't do as much for me as shop windows and the homeless. Only time (and the times) prevents me from returning to the other three points of the program of my youth. But time, alas, has this nasty habit of always moving forwards.

Ultimately, I have remained the urban creature I always was, and my pleasures are those of the city. I grew up walking the streets of my medieval birth city, Sibiu, and I have never tired of that feeling of expectant adventure that's one of the city dweller's secrets. There are also dangers, of course. In my childhood there were the soccer players. In America there are muggers and gangs. But then—I can always run, can't I?

V Where I Hang My Hat

I must admit I dislike
seeing human life
compared to something smaller than itself

making love
compared to a comma

death to periods.
TED BERRIGAN

The beauties
of travel
are due
to the strange
hours
we keep
to see them.
WILLIAM CARLOS WILLIAMS

The Prisoner of Pork

PLUMES OF GREASY SMOKE WAFTED FROM A ROW of sorry-looking tents by the side of the National Highway. Gypsies dressed in complicated rags sold spoons, tin whistles and chunks of meat skewered on black sticks. And then I saw . . . them! APPLES. I made the driver stop, and after he screeched to a halt—every Romanian driver thinks he's Mario Andretti—I bought as many as I could carry in my shirt in five trips. I filled the whole back seat with apples. I would have filled the whole trunk with apples, but I thought of the next sad vegetarian going by and had pity on him. Romania's a hard place on the meatless traveler. One of my traveling companions who fears neither meat nor the dubious source it came from—in this case, a grill that could charitably be described as the lid of a well-used garbage can—actually bought a purplish-black sausage from a Gypsy. I kept my head out the window while he took his first two bites, and then I heard him groan. I turned to look and he had a look of utter horror on his face. He had pulled a ball of hair from the meat. The hair was . . . attached. I tried to calm him down. "They've just had a revolution here," I told him, "they had to do *something* with all those bodies!" He turned very pale, so I refrained from telling him how in my childhood, at least once a year, the police arrested a butcher for turning his neighbors into sausages. It's a local custom. Anyway, it could have been pork.

Pork, after all, is what I'd been battling since returning to my native land after twenty-five years in exile. It had been a rough journey, food-wise. For the Romanian people it had been a rough journey as well, and they had had little choice in the matter. I was on my way to Sibiu, the town of my birth in Transylvania, an old medieval town high in the Carpathian mountains. I had spent the week in Bucharest talking to old friends at outdoor cafés and defending myself best as I could against the slabs of burnt meat with the thin motor-oil cooked fries that garnished them. In addition to these mainstays of the common café there were a number of thin soups with small rabbit meatballs in them that smelled faintly of the grave. I ate pickles, drank a lot of coffee and searched fruitlessly for fruit. One day I ate at a "Chinese" restaurant where soy sauce turned out to be vinegar, potatoes were served instead of rice, and the only available course was the café steak, only this time it was boiled in some kind of evil marinade instead of burnt. The best restaurant in the capital was at the Hotel Bucharest, a grand looking establishment where one gained entry by bribing everyone from the doorman to the maître d' with Kent cigarettes or Bayer aspirins. The chandeliered hall was serviced by tuxedoed waiters who hovered anxiously about the country's *nomenklatura* which gathered here, mainly middle-aged men with many chins and French-perfume scented young women dressed in European *haute couture*. We could have been in Paris or Rome, but we were in Bucharest, and the food, though much better disguised, was still essentially based on the aforementioned steak. I began to think of this steak as the sole of the foot the country lumbered forth on. It's a grotesque thought, I know, but I'm a poet. Anyway, in here I did manage to have fresh peas that were not drowned in mayonnaise like every other vegetable, and asparagus which was the garnish to some viand or other which I left to congeal on the plate.

I couldn't wait to get out of Bucharest and to head for the open mountain country of Transylvania. I could feel vegetables and fruit calling to me from the trees of my youth there. On our way out of the cities I saw long lines of shabbily dressed people waiting patiently in the cold for the nearly empty state stores to open. Next door to these cement state markets there were peasants selling sausages, and even fruit. But few people could afford them. I remembered these lines well. As a child, I'd stood in them at the crack of dawn, before school, ration coupons in hand, waiting for milk and bread. I'd listen to people gossip and I dreamt of the day when I could just stay home and sleep a little late instead of waking in the winter dark.

All my childhood friends, and my school chums had—with two significant exceptions—become figures of porcine dimensions, prime examples of desperate eating during the dark years of the Ceauşescu dictatorship.

My best friend in high school, Ion, was the skinniest kid in the class, but no more. He now disported a royal belly that made hugging him a very awkward affair. In his suburban home in the town of our youth—Sibiu, Transylvania—his wife, also a large and very pleasant person, had prepared a feast in my honor. Dominating the center of the table set festively with hand-embroidered cloth was a steaming piglet with crackling skin, surrounded by a layer of whole fried potatoes, gorgeous chunks of glazed ham which had come from one of the piglet's older relatives, surrounded in their turn by a variety of sausages, including plump headcheese and brain-rice sausage. There were also many small plates of chopped eggplant and pickles, several wheels of *mămăligă* and bread, and I put my faith in these. Placed like guards at fifteen-inch pork intervals were bottles of red wine and straw-wrapped flasks of plum brandy. I had a most urgent need of this brandy, which wasn't long in coming.

We drank several toasts to our reunion, to our friends, to our countries, to everything and anything, so that by the time I sat down to dinner I felt strong enough to confess. "If you don't mind . . ." I said, "I think I'll just have the potatoes, and the eggplant, and those delicious pickles over there!" Anybody who's had to make a radical confession knows the feeling of the silence that follows. There is no opportune moment to tell your friends that you're gay, or your wife that you're in love with her sister, or Romanians that you're a vegetarian. No matter how much good feeling and brandy you'd banked, it evaporates like a dream. It wasn't just that my friends expected me to eat a feast prepared just for me, it was also the fact that they had gone to great lengths to obtain this pig, they had probably sacrificed all their savings, traded one of their children . . . who knows. This wasn't just pork we were staring at, it was the soul of our reunion, the fried monument of our reacquaintance after one quarter of a nasty century. During the time I'd been gone to refine my sensitive philosophy of intake, these people had stood in long lines for everything from milk, eggs and bread. Meat was a rare treat, a hunting triumph in the empty urban jungle. And this meat was mostly gristle or fat or an anonymous bone rejected by the butcher's relatives. Fresh vegetables were practically unknown to the city dweller. Only in the country could one get a good *ghivetch* (a sort of ratatouille) or a mushroom stew or a sour-cream potato or string-bean soup. Only in the country if one was lucky could one get the delicious sour *ciorbas* made from beets or cherries, served hot or cold with a dollop of sour cream on top and fresh black bread. It was also in the country that city people kept their pigs, raised by peasants for money. Several families pooled their resources to pay a peasant to fatten a pig for Christmas. The day after Christmas the entire countryside rang with the joyous squealing of expectant (and drunk) urbanites and the dying gasps of pigs that were then immediately turned into sausages, hams and chops. Children fought over the fried tail, a delicacy. My friend Ion had had the family pig slaughtered for me—and just for me—six full months before Christmas!

The Romanian city dweller of the last quarter of a century had only two choices: starve or eat pig. Those who elected to starve— either because they were Jews, Muslims or vegetarians—survived on gruel and *mămăligă*. Now and then pickled vegetables would come from the country, but rarely fresh ones. And at certain enchanted hours apples, pears, peaches and cherries would make a brief appearance. But never oranges, which were regarded by the populace with the awe of magical fruit. I had brought my friends a bag of oranges that shone splendidly amid the vast field of pork before us. But it was all for naught now, and the feast began in a rather desultory fashion. I loved the fresh *mămăligă* and ate big steamy chunks of it, although it was quite insufficient. . . . a bit like lying down with your bride on the wedding night and nibbling nothing but her breasts.

Mămăligă is a cornmeal bread that's been the staple of Romanians for centuries. It's their pita, their tortilla, their bagel. It can be had either plain in a hardened chunk carried in the saddlebag of your mule (with perhaps a fresh onion) or with milk, cheese, sour cream or smoked fish. It can be cooked with two layers of cheese, a Feta-like sharp goat cheese called *telemea* and a sweet ricotta-like cheese called simply *brândza* (cheese). In the delta of the Danube River near the Black Sea, the fishermen hang dried smoked fish from their ceilings. You open your chunk of *mămăligă*—torn either whole from the fresh baked wheel or cut with a string like a pizza slice—and rip the fish of your choice from the string with it to make a sandwich. *Mămăligă* or "golden *mămăligă*" as it is sometimes called, is the miracle food of the Carpathians. Peasants stir it for many hours over an open fire in a big iron pot. The proper way to salt it is with sweat from your forehead.

As the feast and the brandy began to restore some of our good spirits—though never will I be either forgiven or understood—I tried to explain to my friends the reason for my diet. But how do you explain not eating to a starving man? After all, I remembered well the lunchtimes in our school when Ion would share his raw smoked bacon and raw onion with me on the steps of the chemistry lab. We ate the stuff right off the tip of his pocketknife and it was delicious. Or how about the many evenings of poetry and drink in the outdoor taverns during summer vacation when we ate little hot sausages with mustard until our eyes watered and we had to quench the burning with wine? Something very grave must have happened to me to now reject my past with such disdain. We talked about the fact that McDonald's was opening a branch in Romania. My friend was very proud of this visible sign of progress, but I laughed. There was no way that I could make him see that a Big Mac was not only a threat to the diversity of local cooking (even in its impoverished form) but also funny. "What's so funny," he wanted to know, "about a quarter pound of meat?"

In the end, I got away with breathing in the aromas, and eating only the vegetables and the vegetable-like things that garnished the feast. Romanians have a rich and interesting meatless cuisine, but my friend's house was not the showcase for it.

When I left, my friends begged me to take food with me. This is a custom that tolerates no refusal, no matter how much you might resist it. I call this business "aggressive hospitality." It's a wearying game that can last for hours. Even knowing full well my current predilections they tried to press two large salamis on me. In the end, we settled for a plump goat cheese wrapped in two layers of wax paper and tied with string. It weighed about twenty pounds, more than my suitcase. But it was the absolute minimum. The goat cheese from my friends later beamed powerfully through its waxed layer, causing crowds to part before me. It smelled proud and fierce, smarting like my bruised conscience.

Vegetarian in the Sky

THE TURBANED INDIAN MAN IN THE MIDDLE SEAT
next to me was reading a life of Krishna with colorful plates. I
kept peeking at his book because mine, *Modernity on Endless Trial*,
had the unfortunate effect of causing me to nod out every few
sentences. I was also eagerly awaiting my Continental lunch because I hadn't had any breakfast and it was a long way from New
Orleans to New York. The Indian man's lunch came first, with
his name—an incredibly long name that ended in "krishna"—
written on the plain paper wrapper. The flight attendant had a
pleasingly plump Midwestern face of the kind they describe as
"corn-fed," but I'll bet there was pork in that corn.

"Hindu vegetarian?" she asked, with only the slightest tremor
of disapproval in her voice. It was enough though for the insurance salesman in the window seat to meet her gaze briefly and
raise an eyebrow. They had a meat eaters' understanding: the
meat eaters' secret eyebrow signal passed between them.

The "hindu vegetarian" lunch turned out to be two dryish slices
of whole wheat bread lined with a limp lettuce leaf, cucumber and
tomato slices. The reader of Krishna's life bit dutifully into it.

When my lunch came, it was all the stewardess and the salesman
could do to keep themselves from jumping up. Two in one row!

"Vegetarian?" she asked, reading the plainly typed label.

"Yup, hold that meat!" I groaned, and winked at the salesman.
We may have been of different eating persuasions but we still had
something in common: we were men. We could always wink
apropos of the flight attendant who was good enough to eat. I
mean, he could, and I could watch.

I unwrapped the "vegetarian" lunch: two dryish slices of whole wheat bread lined with limp lettuce leaf, cucumber and tomato slices. I bit resignedly into it, sorrow brother-in-food of the Hindu.

The salesman gloated briefly until *his* lunch came: two dryish slices of whole wheat bread lined with limp lettuce leaf and two round slices of tired, sweaty, fat-pocked salami.

"Hindu vegetarian," "vegetarian" and "regular" all came with identical plastic pouches of mayonnaise. None of us bothered. So much for secret signals; the three of us had a bond that transcended the differences. A limp lettuce leaf lined the dull sky out the window and we were all in it.

Determined to get to the bottom of the food philosophy that created the variously misnamed yet identically crude sandwiches, I called Continental. The general office number was busy for two long hours, due, I think, to the large number of citizens calling to find out what they had just eaten. At long last, a service representative listened to my request to speak to someone "knowledgeable about the process of preparing meals for Continental," and suggested calling the central dining service, located in the 713 area code. A man with a Swiss accent answered the phone. When I asked him about the food, he promised to search for an appropriate spokesperson. When I called again, he had found one. It was a Mr. Richard Quiggle: Mr. Quiggle's secretary took my name and number. When Mr. Quiggle called one day later, he wanted to know the questions I meant to ask in order to pass them on to someone who would tell him so that he could relay them to me. "Is this mysterious process necessary?" I asked him. "Can I not simply speak to the someone or someones who actually slap the glup together?" Only I didn't put it that way because I did not want to spook Mr. Quiggle of central dining, my tenuous link to the mysteries of Continental's cauldrons. "No," replied Mr. Quiggle. So I asked him questions: "What's the difference between vegetarian and vegan in the Continental view? And between vegetarian and others? Who decides? How? What elements contribute to the definition?" Mr. Quiggle appeared to be listening self-consciously at the other end. When I finished, he promised to locate the All-Knower, and call back. He hasn't yet. I am beginning to fear that Continental meals are not prepared by humans, but by aliens with only a rudimentary knowledge of our food sophistication, and no one to explain the makings. I feel sorry for Mr. Quiggle, though; it's not easy to be a mouthpiece for sullen aliens.

On Delta going to Salt Lake City the middle seat was occupied by an attractive but exceedingly nervous young mother. The source of her nervousness sat in the window seat swinging her six-year-old legs with great energy and asking a seemingly endless stream of questions the answers to which did not interest her in the least.

"Why is the airplane standing, Mommy? Is the air better in the back? How do monkeys enter puberty? Is Curious George on this plane? Is there a doctor in the house?"

The exhausted mother delivered a number of answers in a steady tone of voice meant to be overheard by people who might think, "what an admirably patient mother!" but underneath the calm surface of her diphthongs there could be heard a threatening buzz like a chain saw whose unmistakable message was, "You'll catch hell if you don't shut up right now, you little bitch!"

It was not until lunch arrived over Texas that the little question machine at the window quit spewing non sequiturs. "I don't like noodles!" she declared when a broiled chicken leg appeared from under the tinfoil, surrounded by tiny peas and carrots and a small mound of miniscule noodles covered with an anemic red sauce.

The mother clenched the plastic knife in her fist and drove it aggressively into the brat's chicken leg. "You don't have to eat your noodles," she said slowly, "but you better eat the chicken Mommy's cutting up for you. . . . right now!"

That was scary enough to make *me* do anything she said. The little girl obeyed.

When mom's lunch came, it looked pretty interesting: shrimps, scallops, a clam and a slice of fish covered with white sauce. A pineapple slice and some grapes garnished the plate. I asked her what she'd ordered.

"Seafood!" she said enthusiastically, and gratefully. "You can order anything on Delta. . . . low cal, low sodium, kosher, you name it . . ." She was talking enthusiastically as if fearing that the adult lifesaver I had thrown her might vanish and she would be returned to the six year old's world of unanswerable questions.

I encouraged her to tell me all about it. "Well, on the way to New Orleans, my little girl got a salt-free plate by mistake. . . . my God, she didn't eat a bite!"

"I did, too," said the little girl.

"Don't talk with your mouth full. . . . they offer salt free, diabetic, bland . . . it's great!"

As the oppressed mom talked, my own lunch came. It was a vegetarian lasagna with apple slices and salad. It had that solidly-buried-in-Styrofoam institutional look that all mass-produced microwave lunches have. But it wasn't too bad. The red sauce retained the memory of a basil leaf. The lasagna noodles had kept their shape. In the salad, itsy-bitsy remnants of carrot and celery provided brief crunchiness above the inevitable lettuce leaf, which was surprisingly firm. The oil-and-vinegar dressing was mostly oil. The pale little cherry tomatoes reminded me of the fact that tomatoes belong to the nightshade family, so I let them lay there, sad little balls. I did use both the salt and the pepper because this "vegetarian" might have been made by the "salt-free" cook it was so conservatively spiced.

"So you're a vegetarian?" the young mother asked plaintively. The now-sated spawn of her loins looked about ready to doze off, but one never knew for sure.

"Yup," I said.

"Me, too, sort of. Only I'll eat some seafood now and then. The shrimp was not overcooked, amazingly. And the scallops were pretty good. The fish was a bit generic. . . . but what can you expect?"

"Mommy, I want to go to the bathroom!"

I sort of expected that.

A call to United's reservations desk in New Orleans revealed the enthusiastic existence of numerous offers of difference: vegetarian, low cal, low fat, seafood, low sodium, diabetic, Hindu, Muslim and kosher. The agent in charge recited these items enthusiastically and patiently.

"Now only if the people who eat those last three foods would get along as well as the foods do," I said parenthetically. The United representative agreed; in the friendly skies we all fly together with our own food. Buoyed by the United agent; I proceeded to inquire a bit further.

A call to the Delta marketing office in Atlanta yielded the following message for two days in a row: "The number you have called is being checked for trouble." The computer did not say what kind of trouble, but I could imagine: the alien food machine had gotten its low sodium mixed with seafood, vegetarian had leaked into Hindu, the fruit plate had combined with the lasagna. And once again, no human spokesman could be found.

On American to Seattle, I felt sorry for the stewardesses. My seat was right by the food galley and I had occasion to watch them work. The plane was completely full with what looked like exceedingly tall and exceedingly wide people. All of them had a slightly murderous edge to their bodies as if they had been transferred starving in midair from a transport plane. After they had their soft drinks they looked ready to bang their hammy fists on their impatiently extended tables.

It was a brutal job, this waitressing on planes: carrying a stack of heavy trays with a smile, taking back the empties with a nod, carefully lifting another stack so as not to show more leg than is proper to the bulging eyeballs of the road-weary salesmen with growling stomachs. . . . The two stewardesses acquitted themselves gracefully. After feeding about half the plane, they began distributing the "specials." The "specials" were wrapped in tinfoil to distinguish them from the plain plastic "regulars." After taking them out of the microwave, one of them handed the "specials" to the other who checked her list of seat numbers for the recipients, and stacked them in order. They worked quickly and with good humor in spite of the fact that an ominous line had formed behind their backs; more than a dozen nasty-faced doughy people from the front of the plane who had finished eating first and were now hearing the call of their imperious natures. The stewardesses and the food cart stood between them and their goal, and they were not about to stand for it. These were the kinds of people who ate their seatmates when planes crashed. Finally, the specials were loaded and the good-natured sky servants maneuvered their cart so as to let the masses stream into the water closets.

My vegetarian offering consisted of a number of casually sliced and severely peeled legumes, the scariest of which was a huge mushroom with the top suspiciously lopped off. There were also some short celery sticks, dried carrot slivers, about-to-brown cauliflower florets, a cherry tomato and—my enemy!—two clumpy globes of broccoli. A half of green pepper was stuffed with extremely limp brown corkscrew noodles. It looked like a beauty salon urn where the shampooed and still-soapy hair of a giant had collected. A bean dip composed of sublimated beans, onions and hot sauce gaped invitingly toward the celery. A few slices of orange and grapefruit lay innocuously in a puddle of vinegar rimmed with tiny drenched macaroni covered with more broccoli which—this time—was not raw but boiled and smothered. Two ultrathin slices of heavy-grain wheat bread sealed in a pouch lay next to a plastic thimbleful of honey. And all of this, believe me, sat on THE UBIQUITOUS LETTUCE LEAF! (From now on known as ULL.) I don't know what this leaf is supposed to be. A faux plate in case your cardboard plate disintegrates? A backup flotation system? A head covering for Muslims and Jews? Something to dress wounds with? A secret deal with Cesar Chavez? I have never seen more wasted lettuce in my life. Nobody, I repeat, nobody, meat eater, vegetarian or bland fan ever eats this leaf. It is garbage as sure as planes are airborne.

A call to American's 800 number led eventually to the department of food preparation. "You want to speak to our menu preparer, Kathy," a sweet voice told me in the DFP. "Sure," I said, "I would love to." "The only trouble is," the sweet voice said, "that our menu preparer Kathy is on vacation and won't be back for two weeks." There was a pause. "Who then is preparing the menus while Kathy vacations?" I asked. The sweet voice didn't know, and when I insisted, it turned quite sour.

What is one to conclude from all this? That certain airlines care more about vegetarians than other airlines? Certainly, though most of those who don't care would deny it. Or that airplane food, whether vegetarian or not, has certain untranscendable limitations? But then I remember a trip on Air France two years ago when the food was so great, I thought I was flying in a five-star restaurant. Is there perhaps a dearth of imaginative cookery in the domestic kitchens? My own experience suggests that hunger is preferable, and when that isn't feasible, one ought to eat with one's eyes closed while murmuring "this too shall pass," the way one did in one's childhood when mom towered above with an unyielding scowl.

My other conclusion is that, most likely, the foods prepared for us by the major airlines are beamed into the holds of airplanes from outer space. The aliens who produce this fare are not concerned with taste, but only with the chemicals they put in the food to brainwash us. In the end I ought to be grateful that I did not visit any kitchens (if these indeed exist) because further exposure to the stuff could have been extremely dangerous to my health, way beyond the minimal brainwashing induced by the microwaved lunches. On the other hand, I would very much like to eventually interview the deft aliens who slap the ensembles unto the ULLs, but I fear that I might distract them from their work, causing them not only to mix Hindu with kosher or dump too much salt unto the lettuce leaves, but destroy the planet by mistake.

Next time you're on a plane, be wary, traveler! The veggies you're eating may be eating you!

In the Rio of the Senses

THE LIGHTS OF VENEZUELA OR THE SPARKS OF A well-lit Amazonian shaman twinkled somewhere below. I fancied that I could tell the exact moment that we passed over the equator, that magical line that turns the world upside down so that the stars are under your feet and the earth is above your head.

Rio revealed itself brightly as we came in for a slow dawn landing. There were long, sinuous beaches, jagged rocks etched sharply in still-lingering night, modern glass-and-steel towers growing out of each other like a manmade rain forest, and floating over it all was the Christ on Corcovado, his arms open wide in welcome. I got goose bumps thinking about the millions of people below flooding the streets at Carnival time! This was not, alas, Carnival time, but I was sure that the spirit of the city was, on a grander scale, like the spirit of my own city, New Orleans, where Carnival is a continual state of mind, a restless river of sensuality that runs through people, nature and buildings. It is somnolent, underground and nearly quiet in the summer, but it surges to the surface in full feathered splendor at Mardi Gras! New Orleanians are forever jealous of Cariocans (as Rio folks call themselves), for the grandeur and daring of their festival, that unique Carnival, the Latin meaning of which is *carne vale* or, so goes the flesh, good-bye flesh, adios sensual life! And it was the sensual life of Rio I had come to explore. There it is, I told myself, the Rio of the senses, where in addition to moonlit samba dancers there dwell exotics of every kind, unextraditable train robbers, diamond thieves, big spenders, beautiful women, feathered *macumbe* priests, and wild adventurers.

Of these, the beautiful women were most evident.

"Does Brazil need an emperor?" That was the question in the editorial of the *Brazil Post* on May 24, 1991. I had no opinion on the matter, but there was certainly something imperial about my surroundings. The deep blue of the Copacabana sky sat over me like a tent. The Atlantic waves were slightly agitated. They crashed into the beach splashing the nearest lazy bodies. The chunky sweetness of Sugarloaf Mountain (so named either because it resembles crystallized raw sugar or because it's Tupi Indian for "hill to heaven") and the abrupt rocky rise of Corcovado with the Welcoming Christ framed me from different sides. I *was* the emperor of Brazil, seated here at a beachside café sipping a *suco misto* into whose body a dozen different fruits of the Amazon had given up their juices, among them guava, passion fruit, papaya, melon and *mamao*.

I sipped slowly as human beauty strolled by, held together only by the merest strings and the briefest coverings. Everyone seemed conscious of the gazes of others which formed the medium through which they undulated, a kind of specially charged air, but they moved through it unself-consciously, easily, gracefully. There was no hint of that obnoxious Latin machismo of, let's say, Mexico, where men whistle and holler after women. On the contrary, there was a deeply civilized sophistication to the pleasures of ogling, and everything seemed natural. Nor did age seem to matter much, as the old and even the very old displayed what they could to best advantage. Yes, the flesh of those thighs had long ago fallen, but the toenails were painted bright red and the buttocks were buoyed by some stiff bikini fabric. And the men's bellies! Proud of them, middle-aged and old men advanced on the world belly first as if to say: "Here! I have eaten and lived well! Here is proof!" In some way, the variety of imperfection was more fascinating to me than the nearly monotonous beauty of the gloriously tan and flawlessly turned. The young must be perfect and the old must be interesting, seemed to be the Copacabana motto. From this distance, the North American obsession with flat stomachs was *contra naturam*.

With remarkable lack of self-consciousness the beach-clad Cariocans hung out in small stand-up bars on the streets, at restaurant and café tables, in line at the post office. I could smell frying manioc, grilling meats, *feijoado*, azaleas, *caldo verde, pimento de Bahia*, black coffee, bitter chocolate, shrimp, garlic and flavored oils. Café Budapest across the street displayed a dazzling array of snacks in its glass case: freshly made kibbe (spicy hamburgers), shrimp and crab cakes, Portuguese and Italian sausages, cheese, roast beef and ham, and a variety of tropical drinks.

I ordered a *capirinha*, an inexpensive *khishassa* drink crammed with limes. *Khishassa* is a sugarcane alcohol that looks like bootleg "white lightning" and has about the same strength. It had a quick, scintillating high that put a most benign light on everything. A fiercely popular restaurant garden, a sort of barbeque house called *charruscaria* was doing great business next door. I watched a rapid parade of waiters holding skewers with steaks, roasts, kebabs and chicken over the diners' overflowing plates, and refilling them as soon as they were finished. The *charruscarias* also had a fruit bar where exotically shaped tropical fruit was sectionally cut and displayed. I did not see how anyone could consume as much food as the merrily talking and chomping *charruscaria* customers who, with additional affront, looked trim and well fit. There was, I decided, a mysterious relation between the tonic qualities of the fruit that canceled the fat in the meat.

The fruit made me long for Carmen Miranda. I remembered the one-time Vegas star as the embodiment of a kind of Brazilian kitsch that was both touching and timeless. She was possibly the first glimpse Americans had of the mysteries of Rio.

Seated at the back of the Number 119 bus Copacabana-Downtown on my way to the Carmen Miranda Museum, I was holding on for dear life to the seat in front of me as sweeps of blue ocean, jumbled tall buildings and giant flowering trees flashed by. The long blue-black hair of the incredibly beautiful head of the woman in front of me was whipping back and forth across my hands as we plunged first into the darkness of a tunnel carved into rock, and then around a curve straight downhill. I clocked the fearsome transport at about eighty miles per hour, which was about the fastest bus I'd taken so far. No Brazilian bus can be accused of faintheartedness, but this had to be the king of all Rio buses, a bus so intense all the other buses got out of its way and even taxis scurried in panic over the jagged edges of cliffs. Number 119 was being driven by a smiling chocolate-colored Cariocan with flashing teeth who let out great yelps of victory whenever he vanquished another bus or caused a gaggle of lesser machines to scatter. His partner in crime who took the money for the tickets at the back of the bus let out a second yelp immediately after his pal did, so that the passengers were caught in a kind of echo chamber of triumph as they clung to their seats for dear life.

Weaving my way through the intricate fabric of humans thronging the sidewalks in Botafogo, I was hopelessly lost. My guidebook noted the locale of the Carmen Miranda Museum hereabouts, but hereabouts was a surging mass of human beings squeezed by a varied and wacky architecture. An ornate Gaudi-style church with stone goose bumps all over it was tucked like an angel's wing between two massive luxury apartment buildings. At a newsstand groaning with brightly colored magazines I bought last month's issue of *Novo*, a Brazilian fashion magazine, noting that it was three times cheaper than the current issue because of the daily inflation. I wanted to see how different the models of the day looked from the one-time star who was made famous by her fruit-festooned hat. (Rather than by such hits as "Tico, Tico no Fubar.") I then asked the vendor for directions to the Carmen Miranda Museum, and an enthusiastic group of volunteers, including a woman wearing a yellow bandana with fruits painted on it, a schoolboy with race-car driver sunglasses and a Ninja Turtle cap, a blind man with a cane carved from hard black wood, and two miniskirted thirteen-year-old vixens in training, hastened to point me simultaneously in all directions.

Taking my chances on the blind man's directions, I came to a wrought-iron fence decorated with tall bowls of brightly painted wrought-iron fruit resembling mightily the headgear of the one I was looking for. Behind the purples, lemons, chartreuses, and azures of the fence were extraordinarily long candle-straight trees with large brown nutty fruit hanging from them. I entered through a creaky gate at the end of the narrow street and found myself in a dense, cool forest pierced by shafts of long oblique light. In the deep shade at the base of one of the giant trees crouched a little brass dwarf eating a bronze snake, and at the foot of another was a water-spouting naiad with glistening breasts. I touched one of the round fruits on a low branch that I could barely reach by standing on my tiptoes and found this odd fruit to be unbudgeable. It weighed more than a cannonball and it was equally hard. A young couple, entwined in an embrace that was as tight as the dwarf and his snake, sat under yet another of the giant trees wrapped in a cloud of music. A deep-voiced chanteuse gave vent to some deep Brazilian sorrow from a tape deck hanging from a loop in the boy's belt. I suddenly lost all urge for the Carmen Miranda Museum, especially since I was clearly surrounded by a landscape that was very much like one of Carmen's hats but, needless to say, more alive and complicated. As I soon came to find out, I was nowhere near the Carmen Miranda Museum but in a much grander place. A waterfall splashed in a grotto behind an old colonial palace. This was the palace where Brazil's president ruled from until the country's capital moved to Brasília in 1960. It was now a museum, the Museu do Republica, a very serious place that did not, however, lack either Mirandesque exaggeration or tropical excess. The tree canopy made it both cool and dark on the palace grounds.

When I emerged from the colonial park it was to the bright afternoon light of Rua do Catete, and mobs of children just out of school. I sat down to watch them from a small café which was itself watched over by a saint crouching high in the wall above the counter in a smoky shrine littered with money offerings. Two girls were holding forth on the next seats about matters of, no doubt, extreme sentimental importance. A blind street prophet clad in an iridescent green robe with holes in it and a silent transistor radio around his neck preached on a corner to bemused adolescents. I listened to his rising cadences. Rio Portuguese sounded to me full of little hidden waterfalls, namely the sounds *sh* and *dj* which opened up with a soft drop inside every word. "Rio" is pronounced "hee-ou" by the natives. I let the language rain on me. It also started to rain outside, a fast, dense rain that fell lustily on the tiled patio of the café. I love sitting in a café in the rain in a strange city listening to an unknown language.

The sound of that vibrant tropical rain was repeated next day in Jardim Botanica, a vast rain forest in the middle of Rio. It was coming from a waterfall barreling straight down from a huge rock to splash down into a dark pool under a canopy of huge trees. Their branches were full of screeching parakeets and small monkeys. I had gotten to the waterfall by climbing up rocks holding on to huge vines and roots. A teenage boy was under the fall making Tarzan-like noises of delight as the water pummeled him. It sounded like nature was loudly speaking Cariocan. I had never before known what language falling water speaks: it's Rio Portuguese. On the way back I looked at the city spread under me like a handful of precious toys thrown extravagantly in all directions by some capricious child. The tall trees blooming profusely everywhere competed for tallness with the apartment buildings. The *favelas* rose up like boxes that had tumbled from a great height and were now growing out of each other's battered shapes. The sweeps of beach framed every section of the city with sand white, tropical green and Atlantic blue. It was almost unendurably, and carelessly, beautiful.

Later at the Ouro Verde restaurant in Copacabana I began to experience a mysterious identification with the city, in spite of my obvious isolation. I was ignorant of the language, but in some way this deepened the sensuality of my experience because I could experience only what my eyes and my skin told me. There were only a few tables at the Ouro. Elegant and beautiful women sat in flickering candlelight at the other tables with their dates. The windows were open to the sea. The menu said: "We have Swiss cooks." I imagined these Swiss cooks chained in the kitchen, having been captured and brought to Brazil by cover of the night.

But these Swiss cooks make the best of the incredible flavors of Brazilian beef, shrimp, lobster, multitude of fish, and cornucopia of tropical fruit. Everything I ordered, served deftly by the multilingual waiters, was some kind of a challenge to my North American taste buds; the light mint sauce making the shrimp dance, the fish lying sculpturally in the oblong silver dish on a bed of tiny potatoes . . . Having strolled through the mysteries of the main course, I was now staring at a dessert cart of Swiss-Brazilian pastries made from rich dark chocolates, fresh vanilla, cream, nuts and guava. I couldn't go on. I pushed the apparition away.

Strolling through the Copacabana beachfront after dinner, I was very much the emperor, very much the surfeited sensualist. In fact, Rio was catering so profoundly to my senses, spirituality was becoming necessary. I raised my thankful gaze toward the Corcovado Christ in sincere gratitude, but I doubt that he cottoned to the gratitude of overfed tourists. He floated up there in the stars with the great understanding which He no doubt posesssed, presiding as He did over a city of eight million souls, most of them poor, upset by inflation and no doubt incapable of affording the pleasures of the Ouro Verde. Not surprisingly, the patron saint of Rio is St. Sebastian. The Christ of Corcovado may welcome everyone up there in the clouds, but here on earth where all pertains to the flesh, both suffering and pleasure, St. Sebastian, the arrow-pierced martyr, is by far more appropriate.

I felt keenly the sadness of that thought, but I was both too full and too content to dwell long on reality. I dodged a feathered ball thrown at me by a Gypsy, I went past a hawker of emeralds, opals and other precious and semiprecious stones laid on a card table, past displays of Amazon butterflies behind glass, past the African-looking clay jewelry wrapped around bones which was being made on the spot by members of a communal tribe that looked like a cross between hippies and Rastas, past racks of large beach towels on which pictures of the old cruzeiro played with feline bare-breasted beauties under the words "Rio, Copacabana," past a tent filled with Amazon instruments, beaded gourds and feathered bows, a display of mobile wooden toucans painted vibrant tropical hues who flapped their wings in the breeze, fresh leather goods from baby sandals to schoolbags, impossibly tiny bikinis stretched on hangers, past acres of earrings made from feathers, wood, bone, chain mail and silver wire, and past finally, people, people of all kinds, of all shades of tan, dark and black, lightly dressed but mostly undressed, lounging and walking, talking and smoking, playing cards, eating and drinking. It has been long commented how grandly the mixture of races, European, African and Indian, has worked in Brazil. It was true. African pigment, green eyes, blond hair and statuesque figures were not uncommon. The people of Brazil, men and women, are beautiful in overwhelming numbers. My Brazilian fashion magazine, *Novo*, revealed that the handpicked models in there were no more extraordinary than the pedestrians going past.

The cafés buzzed with news (which was mostly bad: inflation, economy a mess, violence) and opinion (the government should resign). Now and then in the shadow of a wall I saw children sleeping on the streets. Everyone brushed against everyone else, their sense of personal space very different from our rigid North American need for a mile of frigid air between us and our neighbors. The Cariocans' bodies shimmered, an infinite wave composed of billions of intimate gestures and movements. Their genuine warmth and civilized intimacy, the sensual richness of their city, were like a warm bath.

"Leave your ring and camera here," the hotel manager had warned me. He told me that "piranha boys," also known as "tornado boys," whirl past one in a swarm and snatch valuables in the blink of a rain forest butterfly's wings. These boys never stormed past me but a thuggish-looking fellow on the beach who sold mystical-looking jewelry made of mud and bones, said, looking me in the eyes: "Watch out who you buy your jewels from! Some of these Brazilians . . . whoosh!" and he made the motion of a swift blade going through the ribs. I felt as if he knew wherefrom he spoke and I moved quickly away.

Paradise is probably a matter of luck. The sun was out for me in Rio, though it was winter and it could have rained as it often does. I could have been mugged, but I wasn't. Instead I was made to feel like the secret emperor of Brazil, a purely imaginary state composed of the evidence of my pleasured senses. When I left, it started to rain steadily, and the beach emptied.

Looking for the Blood Countess in the Bowels of the Empire

THE OLD AUSTRO-HUNGARIAN EMPIRE WAS A punctilious bureaucracy. There was no detail, no matter how insignificant or how horrific, that wasn't carefully noted down in a neat hand. A petty official received seven chickens in payment for his services in assisting a small country noble to find his runaway serf. Noted. "Seven chickens. Serf Found." The found serf received ten lashes with the whip in a public square, and was brought shackled and chained back to his owner. Noted. "Ten Lashes. Serf recovered." This was a small incident, and not one that would cause the thick dust around the report to be much disturbed for the next few centuries. I only disturbed it accidentally because it was in the vicinity of another stack of documents containing revelations of much graver import.

I was on a mission. Nearly four hundred years ago, in 1611, Elizabeth Bathory, a Hungarian countess from one of Hungary's most distinguished families, was found to have murdered hundreds of young girls either, as some have said, to bathe in their blood in order to preserve her beauty, or for occult and satanic reasons. I was determined to find the truth about the notorious Blood Countess, whose story had blossomed into myth and legend but whose life story had been badly told and little researched. The testimonies of three hundred witnesses at her trial had been kept hidden for a very long time, until modern historians located and consulted them. I was sure that a simple visit to the Hungarian National Archives would be sufficient to elicit the documents. I was wrong. The Countess was still being hidden. Everything about her was mysterious, as it had been for centuries.

The Hungarian National Archive is located in an immense building in the hilly area of Buda where the Castle and other monuments of royal power also stand. One thousand years of official Hungarian history are firmly planted in these hills, bearing the ravages of time and war. My rather dour helper, Mr. Janos Angi, an historian from Debrecen, the second largest city in Hungary, pointed out Turkish cannonballs still imbedded in mossy church walls, bomb damage from World War II, and the pockmarks of Soviet tank artillery from the battles of 1956. Some of the heaviest battles had gone on not far from the Castle in the, appropriately named, Moscow Square.

Not many places in Budapest have Russian names anymore. The street names of Soviets have been crossed out. In one of his rare moments of levity, Mr. Angi told me an old anti-Communist joke, and then announced in derisory tones that "there are no more jokes in Hungary. All the jokes are from the old days, from the Communist days." This is an opinion I also heard later from a very important man, the writer Gyula Kodolanyi, who is now the prime minister's foreign policy adviser. The absence of jokes is no frivolous matter. Something is very wrong if people aren't making jokes anymore. In the old days, everyone used to have a smirk on their face as if they'd just heard, told or were about to make up a joke. You could, in fact, trace the history of communism in jokes which were usually the same from Budapest to Ulan Bator, allowing for slight differences. But no more. Capitalism is much too serious.

In the late sixteenth century, when Countess Bathory lived, there was also little to laugh about. War was more or less permanent, the conflict between Catholics and Protestants was lighting bonfires under witches, the nobles could torture their servants as much as they wanted, the castles were drafty and everyone was in physical pain. Teeth hurt, eyes smarted, wounds festered. The only official cure was bleeding. If it weren't for witches' brews, there would have been but bleak misery. Now and then, of course,

Meistersingers plucked on instruments songs of heartbreak and valor, beautiful churches got built, and spring fests and masquerades were called to relieve the tedium. Everyone stayed drunk most of the time. In this light, things have definitely improved in Hungary.

The area of the Castle, where the Archive was, swarmed with agitated tourists who all pointed cameras to the door of St. Matthew Cathedral, a magnificent Gothic structure. The heavily ornamented door swung open to let out a little man surrounded by much larger ones. All the cameras clicked. British prime minister Major was visiting the Castle. Every capital or former capital of the old Hapsburg Empire has a Castle on the hill. The famous Castle in Prague, after centuries of sheltering psychotic emperors like Rudolf, who surrounded himself with alchemists and astrologers, was the setting for Kafka's story *The Castle*, which was a vision of Hapsburg bureaucracy one would do well to read before entering *any* European castle. Most recently, the Castle in Prague was the destination of the aroused mob which overturned Czech communism by shouting, "Havel to the Castle!" Mr. Havel moved into the Castle, wishing no doubt that he was somewhere else, reading a book.

In any case, after skirting Mr. Major and his tourist stalkers, we arrived at the vast facade of the Archive which went on for the space of four or five football fields. Hidden in there somewhere were the documents that would reveal to me the secrets of Elizabeth Bathory who was, some say, a "beautiful woman," while others think that she was far from beautiful, a dog really. In the coming days I heard much more about this controversy, and only after viewing her full-length portrait in the National Gallery at Pest, was I able to form my own opinion, which is that she may have been beautiful but was very badly painted, making it hard to tell. Willema Gizella, an animated French-speaking curator, took me into the vaulted stacks to show me the portraits of the Blood Countess and that of her husband Franz (a fearsome warrior who reputedly enjoyed disemboweling Turks, an activity that unlike that of his wife, was considered glorious). As I stood before the life-sized couple Ms. Gizella expressed her astonishment at peoples' unhealthy interest in the Countess. "Why don't they care about brave and noble Hungarian women like the Countess's mother, who was a woman of culture and skill?" I didn't know the answer to this question, but I asked her if she thought the Countess was beautiful. "The mind is beautiful!" snapped the irritated curator. Her voice echoed through the vast room, but the question of beauty was not laid to rest. Another scholar, an historian, told me later that the question of beauty *was* important because if the Countess had been beautiful she would have gotten sufficient attention so that she wouldn't have had to stick red-hot pins under the fingernails of virgins. A tenuous argument.

Hungarian women, at least on the streets of Budapest, looked quite beautiful. They were dressed both fashionably and provocatively, sporting anything from flesh-colored Lycra tights and black brassieres, to designer outfits straight from Rome and Paris. Elizabeth Bathory, on the other hand, wore a long uncomfortable dress with innumerable pleats and a singular and sad jewel around her neck. Her big black eyes looked into an undetermined future just over my shoulder. Perhaps if she had been allowed to run around in high heels and a micro-miniskirt, she wouldn't have killed anybody.

When Janos and I penetrated the portals of the venerable Archive we were immediately stopped by a policeman. Janos explained to him something that sounded like "this rich American would like to go into the Archive to rip off some of our wonderful national heritage." That seemed to fly because we were allowed up the marble stairs. Rows of heavy wooden doors stretched to infinity in a hallway painted with scenes from the national heritage: kings watching the beheading of peasant rebels, knights walking among piles of corpses while burning castles smoked in the distance, and so on. The documents of the seventeenth century lay behind one of these doors, number 28 to be exact. At long polished mahogany tables, white-haired men and one diminutive white-haired woman stood before yellowed parchments peering into the past. An unshaven fellow in a rumpled suit rose to meet us. Once more Janos explained to him something like "this American was sent by the international capitalist conspiracy to soil our wonderful Bathory." This too seemed to work. The rumpled fellow led us before a Biedermeier cabinet of dark wood and leaded glass and began to pull out ledger books. Written in a small, careful hand, in there were the lists of the materials in the archives. The listings in these ledgers did not follow any order known to civilized people. They were neither alphabetical, nor chronological. The subject matter made no difference either. For the next several hours we searched through these catalogues for the Countess. We found listings of her relatives going back in time all the way to the days when the Hungarians drank the blood of forest animals in honor of the full moon (at high holidays they used virgins.) Their shamanistic gods were eventually outlawed by the pope. The rumpled fellow, who was a researcher employed at the Archive, claimed to have never heard of the Countess Bathory and her misdeeds. Or, at least so Janos told me in the deepening gloom of early evening, as stacks of ledgers piled before us.

At long last, we came upon some letters in Latin from the palatine (the chief administrator) of the kingdom to his king, Matthew II. These were in Latin, but the name of the Countess leapt out, and the year was right: 1611. I asked for copies of these documents. I expected that, at this point, there might be some trouble because the original parchment was frayed and the ink was fading. But nothing in Hungary was predictable. An office boy cheerfully slapped the king's handwriting on a Xerox machine and zapped me a likeness.

Buoyed by success, I was determined to enjoy the nightlife of Budapest. Across the river in Pest, by the fashionable new hotels, the nouveaux riches of capitalist Hungary sat at the expensive cafés along the Danube, making deals. By the glittering entrances of casinos, homegrown millionaires were handing their Mercedeses and BMWs to tuxedoed parking attendants. I had a chillingly expensive drink at the Nautilus Nightclub and Restaurant, a place made entirely out of fish tanks where silk-stockinged beauties practiced English on their polyglot beaus surrounded by tropical fish that swam under their feet and over their heads, while nibbling *blinis* with caviar and octopus Provençale from gold plates. The beaus, who were for the most part paunchy and bald, paid with large-denomination deutsche marks and spoke English with the waiters, dipping into Hungarian only when it was absolutely necessary, like in the marble toilet where the attendants spoke solely the vulgate.

The nouveaux riches have been spouting like mushrooms overnight in the frontier-like feeling that's overtaken Budapest since the communists fell. New glass-and-marble buildings are going up, ancient Empire restaurants are being restored to their former glory by New York chefs, outdoor stands groan with exotic fruit, taxis are everywhere, and prices are comparable with Paris and Tokyo.

A once-popular intellectual, with a large readership, told me that her entire office had been following with great interest the fortunes of her brother-in-law, who started with a vegetable stand in 1990 and now owned two minimarts, two fruit stands and a Laundromat. In the two short years since the grocer got rich, the once-famous intellectuals who helped bring down the communist government had gone from esteem and sufficiency to neglect and shabbiness. Their salaries, like those of other professionals and workers in state-owned factories, are barely enough to live on. The intellectuals watched with increasing ironic wonder the pathetic sales of their once-influential books, and the shrinking of their audiences. This wasn't exactly what they had in mind when they overthrew the regime. They knew that some people would have to be sacrificed, they just didn't know it would be themselves.

After an anguished night of dreams about octopuses wearing lace collars and disemboweled Turks floating about vast stone chambers, I headed out into the Budapest morning which, by 8:00 A.M. was already gray from pollution. The other benefit of capitalism has been an extraordinary increase in traffic, and pollution that ranks at the top among European cities. Budapest's beautiful stone lions, fountain nymphs and gargoyles are having their faces eaten by sulphuric acid. My good friend Janos was waiting for me at Hertz rental where we leased an Opel. We headed out of Budapest to western Hungary and eastern Austria, where the holdings of the Bathory family once occupied large areas. I wanted to see her castles.

Small haystacks shaped like Mongolian helmets dotted the countryside. We crossed the Hungarian and then the Austrian borders with a minimum of formality. This was a small miracle in an area where nothing but barbed wire and armed hostility had reigned until recently. The smiling, casual fellows who looked at my passport must have been the first of their kind to expect no gangs of armed horsemen to come sweeping from the hills that day.

It was a beautiful day, with a mild blue sky. Lockenhaus Castle rose out of the landscape like a Disney fantasy. Restored by Professor Paul Keller, this former holding of Countess Bathory was an imposing city of stone with countless inner courts, chambers, towers and staircases. The Countess was reputed to have killed girls in the upper rooms of the main tower, and I fancied that I could see shapes floating in the chill gloom. From the top of one of the courts I could see the gentle Austrian and Hungarian countryside roll green and peaceful before me. I descended a spiral stone staircase that became increasingly narrower until I couldn't move. A black gap opened before my feet. For a moment, I felt the dread that must have been experienced by a prisoner. Lockenhaus must have been a prison both for its masters and for its servants. It was a complicated torture machine made out of stone, a twisting world of damp tunnels, secret passageways, massive cellars. In the actual torture chamber Professor Keller had assembled some of the Countess's toys for display. An imposing, bigger than life iron maiden stood at the center of it. This was a two-faced statue that opened up to embrace its victim with a number of sharp spikes on the inside. Reputedly, the Countess asked the girls to polish the maiden. When they got close, they released a secret mechanism, the arms shot out, grabbed the girl and the statue closed. At the moment, a number of children were running around the iron maiden, sticking their arms inside to feel the sharpness of the spikes, while their parents took photographs of them. In addition to the maiden-piercing maiden there was a narrow couch with rusty chains hanging from it, two stone balls hanging from a trapdoor, and various manacles, crushers and pincers whose purpose I could only guess. For some reason, my camera failed to function while snapping some of these *objets*, which I took as a sign that the Countess did not want me poking around her domain.

My friend Janos, who had been waiting patiently for me to indulge my fantasies, now gave me to understand that the time had come for lunch. Janos was an historian, but his true passion was food. After two days in his company, I had already divined the permanent motif of our relationship: he waited patiently for me until time came to eat, at which point he steered me toward the most expensive restaurant imaginable, for which I paid. The Tavern at Lockenhaus was a medieval cellar that took American Express. The food was medieval too, consisting of very large sausages laid artlessly on a bed of sauerkraut and surrounded by french fries hewn with an ax from some prehistoric potato. I watched Janos eat these while downing a huge tankard of dark beer. I had what passed for salad.

On the way to the castle of Kereshtur we passed neat Austrian villages that sported many placards showing the faces of candidates in some recent elections with the single word DANKE ("thank you") written under them. These, Janos explained to me, were losing candidates who felt compelled nonetheless to thank the voters. Austrians are, in fact, extremely polite. We stopped for coffee and directions and everyone thanked us profusely for unfathomable reasons.

Castle Kereshtur sat in a field of rye dotted with red poppies surrounded by a chain-link fence. Its gloomy towers and dank structures were closed to the public. My attempts to find a hole in the fence failed. To my surprise, Austrian children had not made any holes in the fence, which was highly unusual. Perhaps people in the area had long memories of the gloomy Countess who had killed their daughters.

The sky, which had been flawlessly blue, began to darken. A rainstorm appeared imminent. At the same time, the Opel, which had been giving signs of weariness all along, began acting in a truly alarming manner. In the middle of a country road far from any human habitation, it died. The only thing that we could see from where we stood were the sinister towers of Kereshtur Castle.

Convinced now that an ancient hex was beginning to hang over our heads like the clouds, we trudged five kilometers to the nearest village. An extremely fat mechanic agreed to view our problem. We rode back as the rain began. Huddled from the downpour under a plastic sheet, he looked doubtfully under the hood. When he lifted his eyes, he proclaimed the Opel firmly dead. The electrical system, especially the battery, had utterly failed. At this point, Janos made his most memorable comment. He said: "Bathory, battery." Embodied in those two words was exactly what I had been feeling.

The epicly sized mechanic proposed that we spend the night in the village and contact Hertz in the morning. In the village, Janos was able to contact Hertz in Budapest. They promised to send a tow truck that would take us back. After four gloomy hours in a tavern that closed firmly and politely, we waited for the tow truck outside. The rain had eased a bit, and the towers of Castle Kereshtur were invisible, but I could feel a rising tension in the air. Janos was becoming hungry again, and the remoteness of restaurants was making him profoundly unsettled. For no good reason, he began raving against Gypsies who, he said, were ruining Hungary. He didn't like Romanians either, and he was most definitely not enchanted by Americans. Could he be possessed by the Countess? I thought to myself. Happily, the tow truck came.

We rode squeezed tightly and silent in the small cabin the six hours back to Budapest. It was 3:00 A.M. when we got back. Amazingly, there were still plenty of open restaurants. Under threat of a renewed outburst of hostility, I agreed that we should eat, and Janos found one immediately. The place was also a topless joint and a casino, in addition to serving expensive overcooked matter in mysterious sauce. By this time, my tired brain had begun composing monstrous images of alien life-forms that were slowly stripping away my sanity.

I resolved not to let the Bloody Countess defeat me. I called up Katalin Peter, one of Hungary's most eminent historians who had, moreover, written a book on Countess Bathory. I explained to her the difficulty of finding the chief documents relating to the trial in the National Archive. "Did you find anything?" she asked me. I confessed that I had found some letters to King Matthew in Latin, and she agreed to take a look. Katalin Peter was a stern, no-nonsense looking scholar who proceeded to demolish all my assumptions about the 16th century countess, one by one. First of all, she said, there was never any witchcraft and satanism involved. Second of all, nobody had any interest in hiding any documents. Thirdly, her own book had been met with great resistance by all kinds of superstitious fools who insisted in seeing more in the tragedy of the Countess than met the eye. Countess Bathory, concluded Ms. Peter, was a crazy woman. It was a sad fact, and she felt sorry for her. But that's all there was to it.

Still haunted by the previous night's dead battery, I was not entirely convinced. "Did you not experience any sort of bad luck?" I insisted. "None." "How about nightmares?" I continued hopefully, "Surely, you must have had some nightmares after reading all the terrible testimonies." "I don't have nightmares," replied Ms. Peter firmly, and stretched out her hand, "Now, let's see what you found."

The historian spread the documents over the marbletop table and began peering intently. As she did so, her countenance changed. At first, she narrowed her eyes, then a look of disbelief came on her face. At last, she went very pale. She stared at the Latin handwriting for a long time. When she looked at me, it was a quizzical, puzzled look.

"What is it?" I asked. I felt quite panicked, without knowing why.

"I have worked for twenty years on this case," she said pointedly, "and I have never seen these letters."

I didn't know whether to rejoice or to run. I asked her what the letters contained. Speaking slowly and deliberately, the eminent historian explained to me that these letters contained a detailed case based on the testimonies of several preachers that Countess Bathory had in fact been involved in witchcraft and satanism. "If I had seen these letters," she said, "my book would have been different."

I sat there in the noisy Budapest evening too afraid to move. Either because I was a fool or because I had been somehow chosen, I had stumbled on a great find. Finally, Ms. Peter spoke again: "You are very lucky," she said. (She didn't know about the Opel or Janos.) "I am going to give you copies of the documents in my personal archive. Take good care of her!"

Next day I obtained Ms. Peter's large archive in Hungarian and Latin. How lucky was I? In addition to now having to find translators for hundreds of pages of documents written in a shaky hand by people from a strange time, I was in charge of a mad countess who had tortured, murdered and practiced witchcraft. On the other hand, if you're a writer, that's luck indeed, never mind the difficulties.

I will conclude my tale with one last incident which, on the surface, may have nothing to do with the bloody Hungarian countess. On the other hand . . .

A consummate traveler like myself knows what to pack. I went to Hungary for a week with my fit-under-your-airplane bag stuffed with the absolutely essential two pairs of jeans, three T-shirts, the one dress shirt necessary in case Important People Invite You To An Expensive Restaurant, and books weighing many pounds, unfortunately. I handed my wardrobe to a hotel maid who brought it back starched and ironed, which is more respect than these clothes ever got in America. Last day in Budapest I went looking for presents. There was nothing either interesting or affordable among the rows of embroideries and fur hats being displayed by faux peasants along the Danube, and I was starting to feel the familiar despair of the untalented shopper who has but two choices: the hidden disapproval of his loved ones, or suicide. It was at this point that I came upon a lonely vendor of honey jars reading a book in a small alley. These jars of reddish Hungarian honey had the honeycombs still in them and they struck me as the perfect presents that would convey at once a message of sweetness, and a certain practical sense. I mean, who doesn't like honey? And the exotic bees who made it were conducive to dreaming of foreign summers in sleepy fields of poppies and rye. I packed the honey jars tightly between my starched haberdashery and the Countess Bathory files and boarded the plane. When I unpacked, I found that one of the jars had broken and all my jeans, shirts and Xerox copies of medieval documents were smeared with honey. No effort at scraping off the surreal toast worked, so I am now working on oddly sweet paper that contains, in fact, one of the most bitter and gruesome tales ever told.

Is this irony or what?

Se Habla Dreams

THERE ARE CERTAIN CITIES AND CERTAIN AREAS of certain cities where the official language is dreams. Venice is one. And Paris. North Beach in San Francisco. Wenceslaus Square in Prague. And New Orleans, the city that dreams stories. Writers come and eavesdrop and take some of those stories with them, but these are just a few drops from a Mississippi River of stories. The Mississippi brings all its stories here from the rest of the country and can barely contain itself from bursting when New Orleans adds its own stories. (The greatest story of them all is, in fact, the tragic love of the old man Mississippi for the considerably younger and swifter Atchafalaya River, a love that the Army Corps of Engineers has been doing its darndest to prevent with locks and keys and cement. . . . all in vain, according to most river watchers. In time, old man river will join his love.)

Ghosts and pirates are thick as the morning fog on certain days in New Orleans. You open your notebook at some outdoor café in the Vieux Carre and find yourself holding instead intense congress with the shadows between the huge leaves of the palm or the fig above you. On certain afternoons light filters its arabesques through the grillwork of the balconies, and you dream without touching your coffee. The dead pass casually by: Buddy Bolden, the creator of jazz, young Louis Armstrong, Marie Laveau, voo-doo queen on whose grave at St. Louis Cemetery there are fresh offerings every night, Jean Lafitte, the pirate, whose treasure is still buried in the fireplace of the Old Blacksmith Shop on Bour-bon Street, beautiful and sad Creole mistresses of French and Spanish aristocrats, old carnival *krewes* and mobs of others, slaves, sailors, adventurers, writers.

Near where I live, there is the Lafayette Cemetery on Prytania Street. Anne Rice's Vampire Lestat lives in one of the tombs. A few decades later, a young poet, Everette Maddox, moved to New Orleans and rented Fitzgerald's apartment. It's still available, cheap, like everything else in New Orleans. There is no memorial plaque. If New Orleans went into the memorial plaque business for all the writers who ever lived here, they would have to brass plate the whole town. There is a plaque on Pirate's Alley on the house Faulkner lived in, but there isn't any on Audubon's house.

When writers come here they walk about smelling everything because New Orleans is, above all, a town where the heady scent of jasmine or sweet olive mingles with the cloying stink of sugar refineries and the musky mud smell of the Mississippi. It's an intoxicating brew of rotting and generating, a feeling of death and life simultaneously occuring and inextricably linked. It's a feeling only the rich music seeping all night out of the cracks of homes and rickety clubs can give you, a feeling that the mysteries of night could go on forever, and that there is little difference between life and death except for poetry and song. Rarely do writers come here to meet other writers. The life about them suffices. Now and then I hear of other writers moving quietly in. You meet them occasionally, but you're just about as likely to run into Walt Whitman, drinking café au-lait and eating *beignets* at the Café du Monde.

The other day, passing the ornate facade of the old United Fruit Company building (the company made famous by the great poet Pablo Neruda's curse on it), I had the fleeting thought that everyone, dead or alive, returns to New Orleans. If people can't come back in their lifetimes they come back when they are dead. And everyone who ever lived here, the costumed Spanish and French dandies, the Victorian ladies of Kate Chopin's age, the whores and ruffians, and the poets, are all still here. In a city like New Orleans, built for human beings in the age before cars, it's possible to move about the streets with ease and there is plenty of room for everyone.

New Orleans is a small city, but it seems spacious because it is always full of people. . . . like a crowded barroom at night. At dawn, a deserted barroom seems small beyond belief: how did all those people fit? The answer is that space and time are subjective no matter what the merciless clock of late twentieth century America tells us. And there is more subjective time and space here in New Orleans than almost anywhere in the United States. Which is not to say that the sad ironies of dehumanized commerce and violence do not touch us here: they do, as Walker Percy's *Moviegoer* or John Kennedy Toole's *Ignatius O'Reilly* amply prove. But the city puts up a fight, a funny, sad fight composed sometimes of sly stupidities and Third World inefficiency. The city can drive a sober-minded person insane, but it feeds the dreamer. It feeds the dreamer stories, music and food. Really great food.

The Muse Is Always
Half-Dressed in New Orleans

I LIVE RIGHT NEAR THE LAFAYETTE CEMETERY where I like to take my friends from out of town for a cup of coffee and a quiet chat. No, you get the coffee *before* you go into the cemetery. Did you think they had waiters in cemeteries in New Orleans? Though, come to think of it, that would be very *N'awrleans*. (As we the nouveau natives have been taught it's pronounced.)

On the uptown side of Lafayette Cemetery, on Prytania Street, is the house where it is said that twenty-three-year-old F. Scott Fitzgerald wrote his first book, *This Side of Paradise*. He had the upstairs apartment, the one with the windows that look on the upraised graves. I can see him, coffee in hand, standing in his robe on the little balcony, wincing from last night's gin, looking down on the little houses of the dead, wishing he was one of them. "It's not so great on *this* side of paradise," he might have said, to no one in particular. No kidding. He hadn't even *met* Zelda yet.

The dead are buried aboveground in New Orleans because there is water less than five inches under the ground and anything you put in there floats off and rots. The rounded mausoleums at the Lafayette remind me of bread ovens: I think of the dead as loaves of bread quietly mummifying there under the blistering New Orleans sun. There is a flesh-troubling scent of sweet olive and night-blooming jasmine clinging to the crumbling bricks.

I took a great Polish artist named Wodycko here one afternoon. We sat on the grave of one Franz Caillou with our coffee, and he

194

told me about a high school student strike he led in Warsaw in 1976. He took all his classmates to the Warsaw cemetery, and they studied history there from the gravestones. It was the true history of Poland, not the lies they were being taught in school. They looked up the heroes of Polish history who were forbidden by the Communists, and learned more in one day than they ever had in high school. That's not a bad idea for *any* school. If teachers brought their students to the cemeteries instead of boring them to death in the classrooms, there would be a revival of interest in history. In New Orleans, certainly, cemeteries tell all the great stories because there are so many of them. There are more dead than living people here, and the dead are not all that dead.

Anyway, after Wodycko and I finished our strong black coffees, we went to the Commander's Palace restaurant to see if we could get in for lunch. Commanders' Palace, one of the world's best restaurants, is on the other side of the Lafayette from young F. Scott's digs. Usually, you need a reservation about three days in advance for Commander's Palace, but you never know.

"Absolutely not," said the pleasant young man in the foyer.

"But!" I exclaimed in despair, pointing to Wodycko, "Do you know who this is? It's Vaclav Havel, the president of Czcechoslovakia!"

The foyer boss looked us over doubtfully for a second, and then disappeared to consult with his boss. We fiddled with our souvenir sprigs of sweet olive, staring at the pictures of Victorian and Roaring Twenties New Orleanians on the walls. He re-emerged shortly with his boss in tow. "Normally," the boss said, "we only do this for old New Orleans families and Hollywood stars. . . . but I'll make an exception this time. This way, Mr. Havel."

When we were seated before the large windows in the upstairs room, Wodycko said that he felt very privileged indeed. A huge live oak stood outside, big enough to live in.

He had the turtle soup. The turtle soup at Commander's is said to be over one hundred years old. They say that the turtle-soup pot has never gone out since the restaurant opened on these premises in 1888. One time, there was a fire and the first thing the cooks did was to take the turtle-soup pot outside. Then the building burned down. There is something indescribably comforting in knowing that you're eating from the same pot with your dead ancestors. The secret charm of old restaurants is precisely this sense of continuity: you sit down where someone sat one hundred years before you. They sat down, told a story, and died. Life goes on. Old cities soothe and ease the pain of living because wherever you are someone else was there before, had troubles worse than yours, and passed on. I don't see how people can inhabit spanking new suburbs without succumbing to terminal anxiety. We need the dead to make us feel alive. In New Orleans they're at it full time.

After we had our soup we strolled back up Prytania Street toward my house. I wanted to show Wodycko my fig tree, and to give him a bag of fresh, ripe figs to take with him to Warsaw where they've never seen figs outside a can.

We passed Bultman's Funeral Home on the way. The Bultmans buried anybody who's anybody in New Orleans for three generations. They are also art lovers and patrons. Frances Bultman, the family matriarch, died not long ago, leaving her art collection to the New Orleans Art Museum. The Museum honored her with a fabulous party at which the dying woman was lain on an elaborate catafalque-like divan as the best of New Orleans society and the art world filed by to pay their respects. Men gallantly kissed the puffy white hand that had deeded art to the city, and women curtsied in their fabulous gowns which in New Orleans are always a little more fabulous than elsewhere. A week later, Madame Bultman died and was on display in the foyer of the Bultman Funeral Home while the same people filed past once more, dressed in somberer hues, but still fabulous. A local *artiste* whispered that Frances looked much better than she did at the Museum where she had been (presumably) alive. Her grand-daughter-in-law, Bethany Bultman, who wrote a book on table settings, whispered into the artiste's ear: "Of course she looks better, dear. . . . All her life she wanted tits. . . . I gave her some." Indeed. In death, the servant of Apollo and Thanatos shone in full-breasted splendor for her admirers.

At some point during her long life, Frances Bultman gave young Tennessee Williams a place to stay in an apartment at the back of the funeral home. Tennessee wrote *Cat on a Hot Tin Roof* there, and liked New Orleans so much he got his own apartment a short time later. The granddaughter-in-law, Bethany, is writing another book, too, on rednecks. "It's amazing," she told me, "rednecks are actually very nice people. I was always afraid of them, but now that I'm getting to know them, I find them very, very nice." Of course, the Bultmans have never buried a redneck, and rednecks couldn't afford to be buried by the Bultmans.

Wodycko wanted to know what time it was because he had a plane to catch in two hours. Neither one of us wore a watch. I pointed out the big clock in front of the Bultman Funeral Home. It's one of the very few public clocks in New Orleans. The rest of them are also on funeral homes. In New Orleans, if you don't have a watch, you have to die before you can find out what time it is. But the real reason for the dearth of clocks is that time is not a big deal here. New Orleans time is approximate: nobody gets to parties for at least one hour after the official hour. Everything takes longer, even the simplest things. Buying a newspaper can take a half an hour if the vendor feels like telling you a story. Waiters may hang by your table, pencil in the air, for the space of several stories if you ask something too interesting. New Orleanians are great talkers and they consider time well spent and very relative if they remember something they want to tell you, or simply feel like commenting on the weather or the political climate (which is spicy in Louisiana, like the food.) Everyone is extremely well mannered, and manners take time to perform and to execute. Nor do stories get carelessly told. My students will invariably preface and footnote a tale while they tell it, and they have a great sense of timing. They may have difficulty spelling some of the words they use but they speak like angels, and for a long time.

Speaking of angels, the Lafayette Cemetery has some good ones, but the best ones are in the St. Louis Cemeteries 1, 2 and

3. Marie Laveau, the Queen of Voodoo, is buried in St. Louis No. 1, and there are always small sacrifices left on her grave: chicken feet, rooster's combs, half-drank hurricanes, cigars and panties. Lately, however, whole tourists have been sacrificed on Laveau's grave after dark, so it's not advisable to visit her during voodoo business hours. Marie Laveau herself is of somewhat doubtful authenticity (some have called her a popularizer and a money monger) but the spooky industry she's spawned is real enough: dozens of books, numerous movies, fetish crafts, sales of charms and amulets, and a great beer, Dixie's Voodoo Blackened Beer. Voodoo Beer, as it's known for short, is the thing to have as you stretch out on your porch.

I have a whole shelf of New Orleans books, and that's about one-hundredth of all the books about New Orleans. If you add all the books by New Orleans writers that are not necessarily about New Orleans you can fill a whole library. A local novelist once told me at a party, "No book set in New Orleans ever lost money." Now, I don't know if that's true, but there is something about New Orleans that makes writers happy. Parties, for one, where you can hear remarks like that. Richard Ford, the Montana short story writer, told me that he'd been living here secretly for two years because "I don't need to hang out with writers. These two streets by my house are enough." I knew exactly what he meant. New Orleans has enough characters in your immediate proximity to fill several books. And if you have the presence of mind—or the *kind* of mind—to remember things people tell you at parties you'll never run out of stuff. People—not just writers—are attracted to New Orleans because it's full of stories and listeners who have nothing better than to listen to them. There is a whole class of people here that my poet friend Tom Dent calls "people who never left." These are folks who come to New Orleans for a weekend visit, or for Mardi Gras or Jazz Fest, and then never go back. Their stories alone can fill a shelf.

The other day, I went down to the French Market to the tomato festival, and they were just about to crown the tomato queen—a young girl from some Louisiana parish—and up comes this older lady, about sixty-five, and she's wearing a big tomato around her hips, and these skinny legs with green stockings are sticking out of it. And she says to me: "Never mind *her*! (pointing to the young queen) I'm the real tomato queen! I been the tomato queen for twenty years now—ever since I left my husband and kids to come here on vacation—I never went back!" And then she said, "I'd love to stay here and chat with you some more, darling, but I've gotta see my other subjects. . . . I still have good legs, you know." And there are hundreds like her, sitting in bars that are really living rooms from the teens, twenties, thirties, forties, fifties, sixties, seventies and the eighties, just waiting to lay their stories on you. In most of America, probably because of television, stories are drying up. Not in New Orleans. They grow in abundance here, like the flowering vines, and the myrtles, the bananas and the figs.

Wodycko was himself beginning to feel that he ought to perhaps become one of the "people who never left." I gave him his bag of figs, and we had another cup of strong New Orleans coffee in my backyard by the pond. A golden-winged dragonfly buzzed a huge lily. Across the street, a half-dressed young woman with long, unruly hair was having her coffee on her balcony. She looked pre-Raphaelite in the subtropical lassitude that began to envelop us. "It's the muse," said Wodycko. It was. He caught his plane back to Warsaw that afternoon, but he regretted it. He's written to me several times since. "I can't seem to leave New Orleans," he wrote, "it's as if a part of me still lives there."

I know what he means.

About the Author

Andrei Codrescu was born Andrei Perlmutter in Sibiu, Romania on December 20, 1946. He wrote poetry in Romanian literary journals under the name Andrei Steiu. He came to the United States on the 28th of March, 1966, and has since lived in Detroit, New York, San Francisco, Monte Rio, Baltimore, Baton Rouge, and New Orleans. He has written poetry, memoirs and essays, and has translated Romanian and French poets into English. In 1989, Mr. Codrescu returned to Romania after twenty-five years and covered, for National Public Radio and ABC News, the bloody coup that overturned the Ceauşescu regime. Mr. Codrescu is a commentator for National Public Radio, professor of English at Louisiana State University in Baton Rouge, and the editor of a journal of books and ideas, *Exquisite Corpse*. He has recently written a movie, *Road Scholar*, which won the Golden Eagle Award.